THE BLOCKCHAIN REVOLUTION

How Cryptocurrency Is Shaping The New Digital Economy

Branden M. Griffith

Disclaimer

I am not a financial advisor and this publication is not investment advice. The information contained herein should serve towards informational purposes only. Nothing herein should be understood as financial, legal or tax advice. The contents of this publication consist solely of the opinions of the writer, who is not a licensed financial advisor or registered investment advisor. Purchasing cryptocurrencies poses a considerable risk of loss. The writer cannot guarantee any particular outcome. Past performance cannot indicate future results. Never invest more than you can afford to lose. You should consult with a professional advisor before purchasing cryptocurrencies of any kind.

Contents

Introduction
A Note from The Author 1

Part One - The Case for Blockchain
Chapter 1 - What Is a Blockchain? 5
Chapter 2 - The Fiat Myth 17
Chapter 3 - The Scalability Issue 23

Part Two - Exploring The Technology
Chapter 4 - Blockchain 2.0 - Platforms and Smart Contracts 31
Chapter 5 - Blockchain 3.0 - DApps 37
Chapter 6 - Interoperability and Oracles 45

Part Three - Entering The Market
Chapter 7 - Risk Avoidance 55
Chapter 8 - Market Trends and Technical Analysis 67
Chapter 9 - DYOR and Begin Trading 85
Chapter 10 - Final Thoughts 99

Cryptocurrency Resources 104
Cryptocurrency Glossary 108

Introduction
A NOTE FROM THE AUTHOR

If you are reading this, you are most likely interested in investing in some type of cryptocurrency or simply curious about what it is or how it works. Regardless of which camp you fall into, by the end of this book you will have essentially skipped or reduced the large learning curve many people experience when first being introduced to the concepts of the cryptocurrency space. I have invested in and learned about various cryptocurrencies over the past two years now. During this time I also gained a thorough familiarity and proficiency in global monetary policy, through the completion of a degree in economics at the University of California Riverside.

However, my initial few months of exposure to cryptocurrencies were spent researching and taking time to understand its underlying technology before I felt comfortable enough to risk my own money. The purpose of my research going into this text will be to teach you everything that I have learned, and compile all of my knowledge and resources, in a simple and easy-to-understand manner. What you choose to do with this knowledge inevitably will be up to you. In these next chapters I will present the information gleaned from my findings in the easiest way to digest as possible. It will be comprehensible regardless of your experience level in dealing with cryptocurrencies.

By the end of this, I hope you can take away an understanding and appreciation for the technology that I think has the potential to shape the global economy in the coming years. Perhaps you can even take advantage on being early to the next big technological revolution.

This book Is Divided Into Three Parts

Part one will provide context behind the need for decentralized currencies and a value proposition for the use of various cryptocurrencies.

Part two will take a more in-depth look at the technology behind different blockchains, the problems they solve, and how they work.

Part three will provide tools to trade wisely and efficiently, while assessing various risk-to-benefit variables that can make the world of cryptocurrency a risky, yet profitable space.

A lot of the terminology mentioned in this text may be unfamiliar to those not yet introduced to cryptocurrency. With this in mind, the language used will be explained as we go on, and a glossary has been provided to reference as needed.

PART ONE
THE CASE FOR BLOCKCHAIN

Chapter 1
WHAT IS A BLOCKCHAIN?

Blockchain technology is the fundamental mechanism which allows decentralized, peer-to-peer "internet money" (or cryptocurrency) to exist and be used in a secure way. It is the underlying technology used in Bitcoin and most other cryptocurrencies. Understanding how a blockchain works will be essential to understanding all of the concepts introduced further along in this text.

Here is what you need to know:

A blockchain is a distributed immutable ledger.

Distributed: A blockchain is decentralized. The information contained on a blockchain is not controlled or controllable by any one entity such as a government. The blockchain does not exist in a centralized server but rather the information is distributed and stored across thousands of computers that host it worldwide. There is no central point of failure. To stop the use of any medium which employs blockchain technology would mean shutting down the network of all internet-connected devices which host it around the world, at the same time.

Immutable: The blockchain is indestructible, unchanging and tamper-proof. Due to the blockchain being distributed across multiple machines around the world, no malicious entity can add, remove or modify any information stored on the blockchain without approval of the network.

Ledger: A ledger is a historical document of financial accounts. In the case of cryptocurrency, a blockchain serves as a publicly visible collection and recording of financial account balances and transactions.

To break this down further, a blockchain is a big database split into different sections of information known as blocks. Every blockchain starts at a genesis block or block one. From there a new block is added and linked to the previous one. Each block is numbered in numerical order and writes new information based on the historical data provided from the previous block. Any new information being added to the chain must correlate to the block which came before it, and multiple machines on a blockchain network must confirm that this information is plausible and correct. It is for this reason that blockchain technology acts as an arbiter of truth. If we apply this concept to a cryptocurrency such as Bitcoin, it is easy to see that no hacker can create a "fake" Bitcoin as it would simply be rejected by the network. You cannot copy or replicate a digital currency on a blockchain as you would an mp3 file on your computer. There would be no history of such a coin being created in the previous block and therefore it could not be written to a new block. Also, no previous blocks can be changed after they have been written as it would alter or invalidate all subsequent blocks.

This process is all secured and verified through a method known as cryptography. Cryptography is most commonly used as a means of encryption and deals with converting ordinary information (plaintext) into a format that is unreadable (ciphertext). This method is used to store and transfer data in a particular way so that only those who it is intended for can read and process it. In relation to cryptocurrency, this process is vital in verifying that a person sending a transaction on the network rightfully owns the wallet from which coins are being sent, without publicly broadcasting the private information which allows the user to transfer these funds in the first place.

Bitcoin was the first widely used medium to utilize this technology and was the first cryptocurrency ever in existence. On October 9 2008, a person under the alias of Satoshi Nakamoto released the whitepaper for Bitcoin. This whitepaper or detailed business model outlined its intended use as a fast and efficient digital currency that allowed for peer-to-peer (p2p) transactions without the permission or use of a third party, such as a bank. Just over two months later, on January 3 2009, the Bitcoin network came online with Nakamoto himself mining the first block and releasing the first 50 coins into circulation. Mining entails solving the mathematical puzzle which links two blocks together, and verifying that the information contained on the new block makes sense when referencing the previous block.

It is no surprise that most people equate cryptocurrency and blockchain with Bitcoin. Bitcoin was the first of its kind, and today, during the time of writing, it still holds the highest market capitalization amongst all other cryptocurrencies. However, it is only one of over 2,000 cryptocurrencies in existence. This is usually the part where a person with little experience in dealing with cryptocurrencies would immediately become overwhelmed. If you happen to belong to the aforementioned group of people who have little experience in dealing with cryptocurrencies, you may be thinking to yourself, "How in the world can over a thousand different digital currencies exist?", "How can you keep track of all of them?" or "What are they all used for?" It is important to remember that 95% or more of all cryptocurrencies have a high probability of failing within the next ten years. Many of them solve the same problems, such as scalability and interoperability, in different ways. Others simply serve very niche markets and have no real use case. We'll cover these topics more in depth later.

This is not to say that competing coins can't or won't coexist, they can, but only the best projects will prevail or hold any significant value in the long run. The sheer magnitude of new projects that have entered the space hoping to make quick money without offering anything of value, other than to capitalize off of the cryptocurrency-hype, will lead to a lot of failed endeavors and lost money for unsuspecting investors. While first-mover advantage plays a huge role in this space, I think we will eventually begin to see inferior technology fade out, while the cream of the crop will take its place in terms of market cap and real-world adoption.

Before we get too far ahead into the logistics of other cryptocurrencies and all of their different nuances, let's take a moment to get a full understanding of the Bitcoin network protocol. It will serve as a foundation for further understanding other technologies moving forward. For most of us interacting with Bitcoin and other cryptocurrencies, our only experience will be with a polished user interface. Most of us will simply be able to press a button or two or scan a QR code, send a transaction, and move on with our lives without the need to know what is actually going on behind the scenes. It is meant to be simple and easy for everyone to use. However, behind this simplicity and ease of use lays complex protocols for processing transactions, verifications, network fees, and encryption.

Explaining all of the different mining algorithms employed by blockchain networks such as SHA-256 (used by Bitcoin) or Scrypt (Litecoin), CryptoNight (Monero), Dagger-Hashimoto (Ethereum) or anything else would be akin to explaining engine timing and compression ratios to a new driver just learning how to operate a car. It is a point of no significance (unless the new driver wanted to become a mechanic of course). I do not say this to mean that any of this knowledge is unimportant, but it will not directly affect your life unless you become a developer or want to create your own coin.

It is important to remember that Bitcoin is not a company, but rather a decentralized digital currency: a cryptocurrency. A cryptocurrency is, as we just stated, a digital currency that utilizes cryptographic encryption techniques to verify and secure the network. This includes validating the transfer of funds as well as protection from attacks. All of these processes operate independently from a central bank. There is no CEO, no employees and no central figure that controls the network. Anyone can contribute computational power to the network (known as mining), and no one has the authority to approve or deny a transaction that is sent to the network. It is a fully permissionless system.

When we speak about something being permissionless in reference to cryptocurrency, it does not mean that we lack permission, rather the opposite. Permission is not needed to complete any action. Normally with banks we need approval to send money to a foreign country, or even when moving large amounts of money within the country when the bank deems something to be suspicious. With Bitcoin and other cryptocurrencies, you do not need to ask permission from anyone before you move your money.

Transactions on the Bitcoin network are digital recordings of the movement of value across wallets. These recordings are all split into individual sections of information and stored chronologically as blocks on the chain. Every blockchain has a block height which is just another way to numerically denote which number block the chain is currently on. All of this data is stored on distributed computers / nodes globally so a hack or loss of data is nearly impossible.

The blockchain serves multiple purposes. One of those purposes is storing all confirmed transactions and allowing wallets to keep track of their balance. Think of a Bitcoin wallet as a digital representation of a physical wallet. The blockchain also ensures that transactions are verified and sent by the rightful owner of a wallet. These wallets are identified by two important pieces of information. The first piece of information is your public key. This is represented by a long string of letters and numbers. Your wallet address is a hashed or shortened version of the public key.

The second piece of information which identifies a wallet is known as a private key. This is a secret piece of data that should be kept safe as it is used to sign transactions from your wallet. Signing a transaction is essentially mathematically proving to the network that you are the owner of a specific wallet. Think of your private key as a digital representation of your personal handwritten signature. This signature also prevents any tampering of the transaction once it has been broadcasted.

After installing a Bitcoin (or other cryptocurrency) wallet software on your computer, mobile phone or utilizing a more secure hardware wallet (more on this later), it will generate your first wallet address and you can create more whenever you need one. It should also be noted that most software wallets as well as hardware wallets are able to generate multiple addresses, and store multiple cryptocurrencies, not just Bitcoin. You can disclose your wallet addresses, represented by a string of numbers and letters (not your private keys), to others so that they can pay you or vice versa.

Mining is a distributed consensus system and is one of the methods which can be used to secure a blockchain. In layman's terms, a distributed consensus system is a voting system where everyone has a fair say in what happens on the network. This system is used for many purposes such as confirming the validity of pending transactions and writing them to the blockchain. In order for a transaction to be confirmed, it must be packed in a block which conforms to very strict rules. Miners then enforce these rules through cryptography. This enables multiple computers to agree on certain protection measures and ensure the security and accuracy of the system. Think of mining as computers engaging in a mathematical race to solve puzzles which link new blocks to the previous block and subsequently secure the network.

The puzzle which links two blocks together is known as a cryptographic hash function, and machines which mine Bitcoin and other cryptocurrencies are essentially playing a mathematical guessing game to solve the hash function generated by a block. This is why mining is sometimes referred to as "solving a block." The protocols used on the Bitcoin network also prohibit previous blocks from modification because doing so would nullify the information contained on all subsequent blocks. Essentially, decentralized mining makes it so that no group or individuals can maliciously control, modify or replace what is written to the blockchain. In order to attack the Bitcoin network, an aggressor must possess 51% or more of the total hashing power on the Bitcoin network. This would entail having a centralized computing power greater than half of the people mining Bitcoin globally.

Miners are also rewarded for their work in securing the network based on how much hashing power they have contributed during a block creation. Think of hashing power similar to how you would an IQ of a human. For humans, this IQ number is a rough indication of a person's ability to quickly solve puzzles. In relation to computers, hashing power is also a measure of how quickly a machine can solve a mathematical puzzle. The current block rewards for Bitcoin are 12.5 BTC split between all of the miners respectively. This reward is halved every 210,000 blocks or four years. The block creation time is about 10 minutes and the next Bitcoin block-halving is expected to occur on May 24, 2020. When this happens, the mining rewards will drop to 6.25 BTC per block. This creation of Bitcoin will obviously come to an end at some point when the block rewards are halved into miniscule proportions. There will only ever be 21 million Bitcoins in existence, and to get into technical terms, based on block halving, the last Bitcoin is expected to be mined in 2140. However, 99% will already be mined by 2036 and 99.9% will be mined by 2048.

Fun fact: For any PC gamers out there, you may have noticed that GPU card prices have skyrocketed recently. This is not due to Bitcoin miners. They use

ASICs or application specific integrated circuits; machines specifically built to mine a certain cryptocurrency. Ethereum was built to be ASIC resistant and therefore uses GPU cards to power mining rigs. Blame Ethereum miners, not Bitcoin miners, for your expensive Nvidia cards.

The mining taking place on the Bitcoin network is known as "Proof-of-Work" (PoW) and is only one of the consensus mechanisms that can be used to secure a blockchain. Other blockchains utilize a protocol known as "Proof-of-Stake" (PoS). Similar to mining, Proof-of-Stake can be used to generate passive income but with the added benefit of not having to purchase physical hardware or bear the electricity costs that mining rigs entail. It is many, many times more energy efficient then PoW. With a PoS system, users staking on the network do not need hashing power as there is no hash function to solve. Rather than paying miners for their "work," the generator of a new block in a PoS protocol is chosen deterministically based on wealth or stake. While this may initially sound like "the rich get richer," different PoS blockchains have implemented rules such as randomized block selection and coin age selection to counteract this problem. There are no block rewards and users staking coins within their wallets are rewarded based on the transaction fees on the network for each block. Staking simply entails leaving coins sitting in a wallet. When these wallets are online or connected to the internet they are known as nodes. The nodes used in this system still have the goal of validating transactions and keeping the blockchain cryptographically secure, but this is achieved in a different way without the need to consume large amounts of electricity.

In order to attack a PoS network a user would have to hold 51% or more of the total supply of coins. This would be nearly impossible for any reputable coin with a high market cap. Also, it would be disadvantageous for the attacker because they literally have to hold a majority stake in the project in order to perform this attack. One of the first projects to implement the PoS protocol was peercoin, and it is now used by projects such as PIVX, Neo and Lisk. Ethereum is also said to be moving from PoW to PoS in a new protocol update known as Casper. It will supposedly utilize a hybrid system of both protocols at first. Not much is set in stone about its development at this time as the developers still face internal division on the right steps to take to maintain the integrity and stability of the network during these changes.

Proof-of-Stake and PoW protocols can also have masternodes. A masternode (MN) is a computer wallet which keeps a full copy of the blockchain in real time 24/7. In order to run a masternode, a user must hold a specific amount of coins and stake them. Masternodes differ from general staking in that they require either a VPS (virtual private server) or dedicated machine to run the wallet continuously. A dedicated IP address and storage space on a hard drive (HD) or solid state drive (SSD) is also required to host the entire blockchain. MNs also differ from normal PoS nodes or even full nodes on PoW protocols because they have a wider range of functionality. Masternodes not only hold the full blockchain and relay blocks but they also can perform instant transactions, increase privacy of transactions, participate in governance and voting, and enable budgeting and treasury systems. The specific functionality and implementation of masternodes will vary between each cryptocurrency, but these are the essential functions they perform beyond security. The rewards allocated for MNs, relative to the amount of coins held, are generally higher than simply staking coins due to there being a bigger contribution to the network. More information on the requirements of specific masternodes as well as expected return on investment (ROI) can be found at *masternodes.online*.

There are still a few other consensus protocols such as Delegated-Proof-of-Stake (DPoS) which implements voting in the block creation process. Proof-of-Importance (PoI) is a protocol which considers a user's overall contribution to the network such as reputation, overall balance, and the number of transactions done through a particular address. These factors are considered by the network to determine how 'useful' a member is. This algorithm was first used in the cryptocurrency NEM. The purpose of all these different protocols remains the same, to make is extraordinarily hard to attack the network, while rewarding those who protect it. Nonetheless, the Proof-of-Work and Proof-of-Stake protocols are by far the most common used for blockchains within cryptocurrency.

For a more in depth look at the actual mathematics behind the Bitcoin network, an English version of Nakamoto's original whitepaper can be found at *Bitcoin.org/bitcoin.pdf*. Also, the public blockchain for Bitcoin can be viewed at *blockchain.com/explorer* for a visual representation of everything we just covered.

Chapter 2
THE FIAT MYTH

Before we go any further, you may be wondering, "Why is any of this important? We already have paper money that works just fine, right? This is just fake internet money that can't actually be spent, and it isn't backed by anything! What if it crashes!" We'll cover all of that and more in this chapter. However, I'd like to ask you something. Can you name a national reserve currency anywhere on the globe that's "backed" by any underlying commodity? If one exists, I am unaware of it. Many times I have seen the argument made that Bitcoin has no value because it is not backed by any physical asset with intrinsic value. News flash, all modern currencies are simply promises by their respective governments that the note is worth the number printed on it, whatever that means. However, this was not always the case.

From 1879-1971 the US dollar was on the gold standard, meaning that the monetary system was directly linked to the value of gold. Americans could literally trade in $20.67 for an ounce of gold; though this also meant that the amount of money in circulation could not increase without the government increasing its gold reserves. Theoretically, this would prevent government overspending and inflation. During the early 1930s the US faced the Great Depression. With unemployment and deflation surging, the US government had little recourse to boost the economy. In order to deter people from cashing in deposits and depleting gold reserves, the US government opted to keep interest rates high, but that simply made it too expensive for businesses and individuals to borrow money. To combat this, in 1933 President Franklin D Roosevelt severed ties between the USD and gold which allowed the government to freely print money out of thin air with low interest rates. Up until 1971, the US still allowed foreign governments to exchange the USD with gold, until President Richard Nixon ended this to prevent foreigners from depleting the US gold reserves.

There you have it, the US dollar is not linked to or backed by any specific asset. It can and has been printed freely (by the US Treasury) through the will of the Federal Reserve without any hard upper limitation. While the USD is still backed by the fact that the US government says that one dollar is worth one dollar; this statement has little to no real-world significance. The value of a dollar has steadily declined ever since its decoupling from gold. Price being a factor of supply and demand, it is simple to see why the dollar has lost so much of its original worth. The supply of money has increased so much that the value of each unit has decreased. Furthermore, we have only discussed one currency. If we look at the big picture, Bitcoin is not just a national reserve currency. It is a global reserve currency. All 7.6 billion of us (July 2018 UN estimates) sharing 21 million coins, minus those that have been lost due to forgotten private keys.

Imagine this: there is a community with 100 people and $1 million dollars are in circulation. There are multiple businesses and jobs within this community but overall there is only a million dollars to be spread around between one hundred people. In a "fair" world everyone would start off with $10,000 (we all know this will never happen but bear with me). Either way, let's focus on the effects of inflation. Let's say that the average price of a good is $100 so everyone can buy 100 goods. If suddenly there were $10 million dollars in circulation, now everyone has $100,000 to spend. The prices of goods will quickly rise for two reasons. First, people have more money to spend and therefore are willing to put forth a larger dollar number for each good that they purchase. Secondly, the intrinsic value of goods will increase as people begin to buy more and competition between consumers increase. This will inevitably lead to resources becoming more scarce. Simply put, adding more money into a closed economic system without a relative change in the cost of production or supply of goods will lead to inflated prices. Using this metric alone, it is easy to see why people struggle financially in our current economic system. Things are getting more expensive and the value of the dollar is decreasing. The cherry on top is that most of the newly created money, which decreases the value of already existing money, stays within the circle of the very people who control its creation.

Let's revisit the damaging economics of inflation with reference to cryptocurrency. Bitcoin for example is a deflationary currency. What does this mean? As time goes on, less and less of it is created due to block reward halving, and eventually there is an upper limit. Only 21 million Bitcoins will ever exist. No hack, attack, fraud, or counterfeit can ever change this. This is the beauty of blockchain technology: an immutable distributed ledger. It is an economic record that can never be altered or destroyed, with no centralized power controlling it. To be fair, a company called Bitmain, the number one producer of ASIC machines (specialized miners), does own a decent amount of the total hashing power on the Bitcoin network. There are more decentralized coins in that aspect, but none of them are as resilient to attack because of the overall power on the Bitcoin network. In order for the Bitcoin network to suffer an attack, the attacker must possess at least 51% of the network hashing power. Even with the eventual introduction of quantum computing, a potential attacker would be battling against the computational hashing power of hundreds of thousands of machines all working together to secure the network, and it hasn't happened thus far.

Fun fact: Venezuela is currently facing hyperinflation due to the over-printing of the Bolívar. For this reason, the country is seeking other alternatives of storing and transferring value, and may be one of the first countries to embrace cryptocurrency as a standard method of payment.

There are two other common arguments used to invalidate the long term success of Bitcoin. One of them is that the Bitcoin network prints money out of thin air and the other is that its price is too volatile to become widely used in place of cash.

Firstly, I would like to address that the creation of Bitcoin is vastly different than the printing of money. The Bitcoin network pays block rewards to miners based on how much work they have contributed to the system. Why do we need miners? We need miners because in a decentralized system, individuals must secure the network rather than a centralized authority. Without block rewards, miners would be providing free security out of the goodness of their hearts, and while that sounds nice, no one does anything for free. So, what happens in the future when the last Bitcoin is mined or when block rewards become miniscule? I believe that in a few years, mining chips and their electricity consumption could be so affordable that miners will be able to sustain themselves on the network transaction fees as well as a rise in price level.

Secondly, the volatility in the price of Bitcoin is due to its small market cap and volume relative to other asset classes. What Bitcoin needs is mass adoption which leads to liquidity. Liquidity means there are a large number of players in the market, such that it is easy to buy and sell and that no one player is big enough to shift the market upward or downward. Adding on to that, Bitcoin does not need to be used as cash in order for it to survive. Gold for example is not used as cash for everyday purchases but is widely considered a valuable commodity. While Bitcoin does share some similar qualities to that of gold in terms of scarcity, it also eliminates many of gold's problems. Gold is heavy to carry around, easy to steal or confiscate, and is not easily or near infinitely divisible. Bitcoin on the other hand is divisible down to eight decimal places and has no physical representation. In that aspect, it is even better positioned to be used much more frequently than Gold in everyday transactions.

Perhaps people may only see it being advantageous to part with their coins for larger purchases such as cars or even homes rather than groceries or movie tickets. Perhaps fiat money will not be replaced immediately, but rather coexist with a cryptocurrency other than Bitcoin. It may also be possible that fiat money will be replaced fully by a small handful of different coins respective to what each country or region in the world prefers to use. It is not yet clear whether Bitcoin will be the dominant currency in terms of small purchases such as coffee. It could end up just being used for larger and more infrequent purchases, while a different coin or coins are used for more common everyday activities. Perhaps the scarcity of Bitcoin itself will hinder its use in everyday purchases in favor of a cryptocurrency with a higher circulating supply. In any case, it should be made clear that it is not a requirement to have everyone using Bitcoin for day-to-day purchases for it to maintain value, any more than everyone needs to own gold or use gold to buy their coffee for it to maintain value. Bitcoin is better positioned than gold to do both, but does it have to be used that way to maintain its value? No. All it needs is liquidity.

As I am writing this, Facebook recently had its largest crash to date after its July 2018 earnings and user growth report fell slightly below projections. They lost a total of about $146 billion in market cap. This is larger than the entire current market cap of Bitcoin itself at $141 billion (with a price of $8,200 and a circulating supply of 17.1 million). This is just the intraday fluctuation of one company, not to forget that the market cap of the entire global stock market is around $73 trillion. What I am trying to say is that we are still very, very early.

Chapter 3
THE SCALABILITY ISSUE

One of the biggest problems plaguing Bitcoin and other cryptocurrencies is known as the scalability issue. On an average day, the payment processor Visa handles about 150 million transactions. This works out to around 1,700 transactions per second (TPS). The Bitcoin network can currently only process around 7 transactions per second. We haven't even mentioned Mastercard, American Express, Union Pay or any other massive payment processor, and already we can see that Bitcoin is at an astronomical disadvantage. We have not yet reached any use levels near mass adoption, and still the Bitcoin network has been clogged numerous times, with transactions often taking multiple hours while the network is busy. Below I will discuss some of the many solutions implemented in Bitcoin and other cryptocurrencies in order to address this issue.

Forks

There are two types of forks a cryptocurrency such as Bitcoin can undergo. The first type is a soft fork and the second type is a hard fork. A fork is simply a change in the network protocol consensus. One of the most recent and talked about soft forks on the Bitcoin network is known as Segwit or segregated witness. Many times

Litecoin will act as a sort of lab rat for new protocol experimentation so it received the upgrade first on May 10 2017, while Bitcoin received it on August 23rd of the same year. Segwit essentially removes the signature or "witness" from the base transaction block. This protocol change is sort of an accounting trick which allows the witness data not to be counted against the block size. As a result, individual transaction data is interpreted to be smaller and therefore more points of activity can be stored on a single block. In other words, more transactions are confirmed and stored in each block, allowing for higher TPS without changing the block size. Due to the block size remaining the same, the activation of Segwit is backwards compatible with the previous protocol of the blockchain on which it is implemented, so there is no need for a hard fork.

The original idea behind the Segwit upgrade was not seeking to be a scaling solution. Rather, it aimed to fix a bug called transaction malleability. This bug allowed anyone to change small details in the transaction id and its subsequent hash, but not the content within the transaction itself. Even though this was a small flaw, it prohibited second-layer features and smart contracts due to security issues. With Segwit removing the signature or witness from the base transaction block, it allowed signatures and scripts to be modified without altering the transaction id. We will come back to why this is important soon.

One of the biggest and most heated debates within the crypto-community is the debate between Bitcoin (BTC) and Bitcoin Cash (BCH). In opposition to the upcoming Segwit implementation, Bitcoin Cash was forked from Bitcoin on August 1st 2017 at block #478,558. This took place just a few weeks before the Segwit soft fork was activated. Bitcoin Cash takes an opposite approach to the block size limitation. Rather than trying to reduce individual transaction sizes, the Bitcoin Cash fork chose to increase Bitcoin's block size from 1mb to 8mb, with room for even bigger block production down the line. To simplify things, I like to think of this comparison in terms of traffic on a highway. Bitcoin creates smaller cars while Bitcoin Cash widens the highway.

Supporters of Bitcoin Cash often refer to Bitcoin as "Bitcoin Core," attempting to discredit its authority and proclaim Bitcoin Cash as the "real Bitcoin." I think that this practice is harmful insomuch that it may confuse first time investors on what they are actually buying. However, most people in the community still accept Bitcoin (BTC) as the real Bitcoin and do not use the "core" moniker. There are valid arguments from each side of the spectrum on the "right" way to scale a blockchain. However, I will not get into this topic too much because it is a rabbit hole for argumentation within the community. Just know that Bitcoin (BTC) is the original Bitcoin and Bitcoin Cash (BCH) is a fork of this. One implements the use of Segwit and allows for smaller transaction sizes, as well as second-layer scaling solutions down the line, while the other uses bigger block sizes.

Other less-popular forks of Bitcoin include but are not limited to, Bitcoin Diamond, Bitcoin Private, Bitcoin XT, Classic, Gold, Unlimited and the list goes on. Just scroll through Coinmarketcap and you will find Bitcoin X, Y and Z all having slightly different characteristics to their blockchain protocols. Bitcoin forks are distributed to those who hold Bitcoin (BTC) relative to the amount which they hold. In my humble opinion, forks are negatively impacting Bitcoin by splitting the consensus within the community; but only inasmuch as people are willing to try and capitalize on the current market hype of receiving "free money" from these forks. In the long run, I believe the better technology will come out on top, whatever that may be. However, at this current point in time much of the market is driven by speculation and hype.

Fun Fact: A common misconception in the cryptocurrency space is that Litecoin is a fork of Bitcoin. While Litecoin utilizes a modified source code of Bitcoin, it is not actually considered a fork because its blockchain history is not shared. It started off as a completely new chain, and its existence began off of its own genesis block. It has a much faster block generation time at 2.5 minutes, rather than 10 minutes for Bitcoin. This allows it to reach 28 TPS but with Segwit implementation it can achieve 56 TPS. TPS is variable based on the block size, the size of each transaction within a block and the block generation time. For example, let's say that a block is 2.5mb and a new block is generated every 5 minutes. If the average transaction size is 1kb then each block will hold 2,500 transactions. Sixty seconds multiplied by five is 300, then we divide 2,500 transactions by 300 seconds which gives us an average of about 8.3 TPS.

Second Layers

Currently, one of the biggest developments within the cryptocurrency community is known as the Lightning Network (LN). The activation of Segwit comes into play here because it eliminates the risk of transaction malleability. The Lightning Network works by adding a "second-layer" to the Bitcoin network by allowing users to create payment channels. To do this, two entities who wish to transact with one another must open a multisig or multiple signature wallet (this requires more than one signature to enact a transaction). This wallet will hold some amount of Bitcoin and its address is stored on the blockchain. The two parties are now able to conduct as many transactions as they would like without relaying any of this information to the blockchain. These transactions are known as "off-chain" transactions because they are not written to the blockchain and are usually small transfers of value. After every transaction, both parties sign off on an updated balance sheet which denotes how much funds being stored in the wallet belong to each person. When both parties are done transacting, the channel can be closed and the final balance is then recorded on the blockchain. Both parties are entitled to their share of the wallet based on the latest updated balance sheet.

Lastly, it is important to note that you do not have to set up a direct channel to transact on the LN. You can send or receive payments via channels with people who you are already connected with and the network will automatically find the shortest route to transact with the intended person. The current two bottlenecks to the LN are the use of Segwit-enabled wallets to run secure payment channels, and the development and use of lightning wallets and open channels on the network itself. The more lightning channels that are open on the LN, the easier it will be to transact with someone because the network will form a mesh of connections to different parties. If all of this sounds too confusing to integrate into your daily life, just know that the version which you will most likely use will be a polished app with a few buttons to press. Most people using it will never know what is going on in the background.

One big advantage of the LN is that because transactions take place between individuals on private channels, they do not need to be broadcasted to the entire network and are therefore instantaneous. No one except the two parties transacting need to verify what is happening inside a payment channel. Another side effect to this, is that there are little to no network fees because nothing is being written to the blockchain. However, to that same note, because the Lightning Network forgoes the security of the blockchain, it is not as secure and thus will mostly be used only for small purchases or micropayments. Larger movements of value will be more suited for the decentralized security that the main blockchain offers. Hopefully, the LN will alleviate some of the pressure off of the Bitcoin network as more on-chain scaling solutions are developed for the main blockchain. Other coins such as Stellar, Litecoin, Vertcoin and Decred among many others, are also planned to utilize the Lightning Network. This will enable more payment options and also allow users to settle payments in different currencies, other than the ones they have sent with. Additionally, other projects have been developing their own scaling solutions as an alternative to the LN. For example, Ethereum and Neo are developing Raiden and Trinity respectively as off-chain scaling solutions.

PART TWO
EXPLORING THE TECHNOLOGY

Chapter 4
BLOCKCHAIN 2.0 - PLATFORMS AND SMART CONTRACTS

With the cryptocurrency space growing so rapidly, why doesn't every existing company or project wanting to create a name for itself just create their own blockchain? Well first of all, as a consumer, imagine needing tens or even hundreds of unique wallets just to utilize all of the services that could potentially be a part of our daily lives. It would seem insane and impractical that so many different projects and companies would utilize different blockchains and all require unique wallets. Not only would this be very fragmented and impossible to keep track of, it would also be extremely expensive for individual companies (especially startups) to code and produce a secure and reliable blockchain protocol. This is where Blockchain 2.0 comes in. Platforms allow for numerous companies to utilize the same decentralized cryptographic technology, without having to build it from scratch themselves. The most notable and successful cryptocurrency since Bitcoin is Ethereum, and some would even say it has a greater use case.

Ethereum is a platform which utilizes smart contracts, upon which other projects can also be built. Let's break this down into its two parts. The Ethereum blockchain can host other tokens which makes it easier for various projects and companies to create a digital piece of value in their ecosystem. The term tokens and coins are often used interchangeably in the cryptocurrency space but there are some key differences. Coins which act solely as a currency or store of value are referred to as just coins. For example: BTC (Bitcoin), LTC (Litecoin), or XMR (Monero). Tokens on the other hand are hosted on a platform such as Ethereum and provide a use beyond that of a simple digital currency. For example, holding tokens for various projects may provide the user with access to certain features on said platform. Many exchange-issued tokens (exchange tokens) may promise buybacks, reduced trading fees or even dividends from trading. Others may grant community voting rights for future business decisions or even technical changes within the platform.

As we mentioned, the other half of blockchain 2.0 consists of smart contracts. Smart contracts are essentially the same as real-world contracts except they are digital. They are built to execute an action once a certain set of requirements are fulfilled. The contracts themselves are small programs which sit within the blockchain and are visible and verifiable by all parties interacting with it.

Think of a platform such as Kickstarter. Companies present a project on the Kickstarter platform and based on the validity of each project, users donate money to fund the startup's new idea. However, before this money reaches the startup, it must go through a third party: Kickstarter. We have to trust that Kickstarter will do the right thing and distribute the money appropriately after fees. With smart contracts, we have the ability to essentially remove this intermediary. A smart contract can be written to collect a certain amount of money. If that goal is reached, it is released to the creators. If the goal is not reached, it is sent back to the funders accordingly. It can also be written to release the money to the creators and still give tokens to the supporters regardless of if a goal is reached or not. They can be programmed to do almost anything.

Smart contracts are also immutable, which as we discussed in previous chapters, means that the code cannot be tampered with once it has been set. No one can steal or hack money from a smart contract because it lives on the blockchain. Furthermore, smart contracts can have much greater and more complex uses than being mechanisms for fundraisers. They can be coded to perform tasks in almost any application such as banking via loans or automatic payments, paying out insurance claims, or even triggering postal delivery payments, to name a few of the possibilities.

Going back to using smart contracts for fundraising; cryptocurrency markets have many startups which are funded through ICOs. An ICO is known as an initial coin offering and is similar to an IPO or initial public offering when a company goes public with their stock. The technical process is as follows. Create an ERC20 token and deploy a smart contract set to issue those tokens at a specified ratio. The company receives Ether based on how much is sent to their smart contract and the supporters receive tokens which will "supposedly" have a use case and increase in value based on what the project creates. There are quotes around the word supposedly because many of the ICOs in 2017 have largely been unsuccessful for many reasons. We will cover this in more detail later on.

So what are these "tokens" that can be built on Ethereum? Well, they are referred to as ERC tokens which is short for Ethereum Request for Comment.

These are technical guidelines or protocols used to build standards on the Ethereum platform. To create standards for the Ethereum platform a developer submits an EIP or Ethereum Improvement Proposal. The proposal includes a feature rationale, technical specification and contract standards. Once an EIP is reviewed, approved by a committee and finalized, it becomes an ERC. The list of current EIPs can be found at *github.com/ethereum/EIPS*. Below I will elaborate on the most common ERC token standards and their functionality.

ERC-20: This Ethereum token is used for fungible / interchangeable assets. ERC20 tokens are exact replicas of one another. One OmiseGo token = one OmiseGo token. This is by far the most popular standard to date and has been used in hundreds of ICOs.

ERC-721: Proposes a concept where token holders can differentiate between the tokens they hold. These are non-fungible tokens which can be used represent unique items or characteristics. Also, because these tokens are unique and non-fungible, they can potentially be used to tokenize any unique object in the real-world such as cars or real estate.

ERC-1155: Similar to the ERC721 token with a few improvements. Current token designs require that a separate smart contract be sent out for each token type. In layman's terms, this is like having to purchase each grocery separately at the store checkout line. Imagine having to swipe your debit card for each item, bag a separate loaf of bread, separate milk, separate cheese, separate bananas etcetera and then getting a separate receipt for each item. The ERC1155 token allows users to send up to 200 tokens at a time and perform complex bundled operations. It also enables users to move fungible, semi fungible and non-fungible tokens using a single suite of smart contracts.

ERC-223: Fixes one of the main problems with ERC20 tokens, token fallback. For example, if Ether is sent to a smart contract not meant to handle Ether, it will get rejected and sent back to the original address it was sent from. However, if an ERC20 token gets sent to a wrong contract address that is not written to accept a certain token, it can get stuck. The ERC223 standard provides token fallback in case of an incorrect transfer. These tokens also have the advantage of only using half of the normal gas fees and minimize blockchain bloating.

ERC-827: Upgrade to the ERC223 standard but also provides the functionality of adding a transfer of data. This data can be used to trigger a second smart contract which executes a function or allows an additional action to take place.

ERC-621: Extension of the ERC20 standard which adds two additional functions: increasesupply and decreasesupply. The ERC20 standard only allows a single token issuance, which caps the total supply of tokens at a fixed number. The ERC621 standard proposes that total supply can be modified.

Fun fact: In 2017 a game called Crypto Kitties came out of the ERC721 token standard. This game allowed players to exchange unique virtual cats in the form of ERC721 tokens. It has been recorded that some of these collectible cats have sold for over six-figures

Let this not be your end-all be-all for knowledge on blockchain 2.0, but simply a foundation and framework for which to understand and analyze other projects. Some other platforms which provide similar functionality to Ethereum are Lisk, Waves, Eos, Neo (referred to as the Chinese Ethereum) and ICON (referred to as the Korean Ethereum). Note that I mention these projects not out of support or consignment (in other words, not investment advice) but only so much that they represent blockchain platforms with smart contract functionality similar to that of Ethereum. For example, the NEP-5 token built on Neo can be compared to the ERC-20 token on Ethereum. All of these platforms provide gateways for which other companies can build upon. They all have ever-evolving token standards and protocol upgrades.

Chapter 5
BLOCKCHAIN 3.0 - DAPPS

Blockchain 3.0 is regarded to be the advancement of DApps, otherwise known as decentralized applications. This technology pushes the limits of cryptography beyond just smart contracts and can create use cases in areas such as health, education, gaming, arts, entertainment, sciences and even government. The advantage that DApps have over traditional apps is that their backend code does not live on centralized servers. Rather, their code lives and relies on a decentralized p2p network such as Ethereum, which guarantees transparency. Think of a DApp as you would an application from the Apple App Store or the Google Play Store. They are similar in functionality, but rather than being written for Apple or Android, they are written for Ethereum, Neo, or any other decentralized platform. Since the code for these DApps lives on a public blockchain, supported by thousands of computers worldwide, it is visible and verifiable for anyone to see which adds a layer of trust and transparency. Also, no one can restrict the use of any application on the blockchain.

With the advancement of smart contracts, tokens, and DApps, came one of the biggest investment opportunities seen in a long time: the ICO. We already stated that an ICO is a fundraiser for a startup, but the ability to invest in this way in legacy stock markets has long been restricted from the general public. For participants in the US stock market, in order to invest in a startup, a person must first be an accredited investor. At face value, this may seem like the government is protecting those with little trading experience from getting burned. However, once we look deeper into this, the accredited investor law simply states that, "you must first be rich, in order to become richer." The barrier to becoming an accredited investor entails having a net worth of over $1 million, not including your home. I find this to be an egregious violation of the "American Dream," considering that US citizens spent $73.5 billion annually on lottery tickets (2016). The Powerball only paid out $700 million, of which much was paid back into taxes. Nonetheless, this represents a -99.04% return on investment overall for the American public. The rich are allowed to privately participate in some of the most lucrative investment opportunities such as hedge funds, venture capital funds and private equity, while the poor are left only to gamble.

There was a big ICO boom throughout much of 2017, with many of them promising bigger than life technological advancements. Investors from all over the world were throwing ETH at just about any company with a whitepaper and a halfway decent designed website. As a result of this, every week various hyped ICOs raised multi-million dollar figures worth of Ether in a matter of minutes. This hype also resulted in many projects returning gains unheard of in traditional markets. It was not uncommon for any run of the mill project to give investors anywhere from 5x to even 100x or more returns from ICO price within a few weeks or months. It should be noted though, that things are far from perfect within the ICO world. About a year later, a big majority of these projects have yet to release a working product, or have a released something that is a far cry away from what was originally promised. While it is important to remember that nothing great is built in a day (google a picture of the first version of Amazon), the disconnect between what is promised vs what is actually delivered has been a huge strike to the overall credibility of the ICO space as well as the cryptocurrency space in general. Perhaps this will improve as time goes on, though the current state of DApps and ICO projects in general is nothing close to what was promised by a majority of companies.

The fallout of many underperforming projects, and projects which turned out to be blatant scams, caused a lot of noise within the cryptocurrency world. Many regulatory bodies decided to crack down on these token offerings. Most notably in the US was the Securities and Exchange Commission (SEC). The SEC has, for the time being, deemed that tokens issued through ICOs be considered securities. They have also demanded that any company conducting an ICO must have it registered through them, or prohibit the sale of tokens to US investors. Much of the "ICO-mania" has died down in recent times, largely due to this regulation and grey-area regarding what legal jurisdiction the SEC has over digital currencies.

John McAfee, known widely as the father of internet security, is a British-American computer programmer responsible for the McAfee antivirus software. He is also, as of recent, a very outspoken figure in the crypto-community. His opinion on this topic is that the SEC is grossly overstepping their bounds, stating in an interview that "There is no legislation that can protect you from yourself." He also went on to say that "Truth and regulation cannot coexist" when referencing blockchain technology and centralized governments imposing their legislation on various decentralized networks.

I tend to agree with this sentiment, in that it stifles innovation for US-based blockchain projects and also places US investors at a large disadvantage. John McAfee expects that ICOs will return in popularity for US investors in the future when the market matures, but perhaps under the framework of an initial loan procurement (ILP). An ILP would only involve token based loans with the promise of a future buyback, which definitively falls outside of the SECs jurisdiction. Whatever the case may be, the ICO space is still an area of much uncertainty in the crypto-community. This ambiguity may improve over time, given that there is a revision of current regulations, or a shift in the structure of ICOs themselves.

Fun fact: The legal ambiguity of cryptocurrency in America does not stop with ICOs. At this current point in time, the Internal Revenue Service (IRS) classifies cryptocurrency as property, while the Commodity and Futures Trading Commission (CFTC) classifies it as a commodity.

While many of the projects that were promised in 2017 have not yet came into fruition at the time of writing, I would like to take some time to briefly cover a few which either do have a working product or hold a decent amount of credibility within the community, to give you an idea of some of the possibilities that exist within this space.

One notable project that has been developed with a working DApp is Golem. Golem in short is an Airbnb for computers. It is a platform for decentralized supercomputing that allows users to loan out or buy computational power. The Golem platform allows other computers, which may not have as robust hardware capabilities on their own, to run intensive programs such as the 3D modeling studios or other graphic intensive applications. Perhaps it could even be utilized by big film studios to quickly render a VFX-heavy scene. Users on the platform are paid in the native Golem (GNT) token which can be purchased from various exchanges.

0x is an open protocol for building decentralized exchanges on the Ethereum platform. This protocol utilizes smart contracts and will allow anyone to operate a decentralized exchange. A decentralized exchange allows users to safely trade ERC tokens without the need to place their funds in the custody of a centralized exchange. 0x is different from other decentralized exchanges as they will not charge any fees for trading. They also plan to avoid network fees and slow speeds by relaying orders off-chain and will only bring them back on-chain when they need to be settled.

Walton Chain is perhaps one of the most ambitious DApps and utilizes multiple technologies. Unlike Golem and 0x, it is not an ERC20 token and runs on its own blockchain. In short, Walton is a project that combines blockchain technology with Radio-Frequency IDentification technology (RFID) to improve supply chain management. They are currently based in Korea and target the clothing and manufacturing industry. They offer decentralized product management by tracking QR and RFID codes on the blockchain. This can be implemented for uses such as tracking in-store retention rates once a customer picks up or tries on an item, to making a purchase. It can also be used to track the authenticity of a certain item and its manufacturing origin to identify counterfeit products, among other things.

One of the biggest bottlenecks of DApps is again, the scalability issue. We have already mentioned the ERC721 token and the game Crypto Kitties which implemented the use of non-fungible tokens. (This game is also a DApp.) As funny as it may sound, at its release in mid 2017 this game actually clogged up the Ethereum network, resulting in very high gas fees as well as long transaction times. Even popular ICOs can sometimes clog the network and cause long transaction times, as thousands of people send Ether to a single smart contract at once.

Ethereum currently runs at about 15-20 TPS and plans to scale to a million through a technology known as sharding. It is an on-chain or layer one scaling solution and works by dividing the blockchain network into fragments, referred to as shards. These shards contain their own piece of state and transaction history independently. These pieces are then given their own group of nodes which are responsible for processing certain information fragments. This optimizes and accelerates the process of confirming transactions because not all nodes on the blockchain network are required to process every piece of data written to it.

I like to think of sharding as dividing a workload or delegating the responsibilities into a group project. It is more efficient for multiple people to handle independent tasks and work on them at the same time, rather than having everyone work on the same part all at once. Vitalik Buterin, creator of Ethereum, said in an interview that the idea of "quadratic sharding" which layers the same structure on top of itself, is the key to reaching millions of transactions per second. If we go back to the simple example of traffic on a highway, I like to think of sharding as building multiple highways on top of one another, which all travel in the same direction.

Neo is working on its own on-chain scaling solutions as well, known as neo-sharp and HyperVM, and plans to reach 100,000 transactions per second by 2020. Again, these are separate from second-layer or off-chain scaling solutions which are not written to the main blockchain. If we are comparing cryptocurrency to the internet, I like to think we are still in the dial-up phase. We have yet to develop DSL, wireless modems, fiber optics, mobile networks such as 2G, 3G, 4G or 5G and all of the intricate websites, applications and resources that are accessible using this technology, none of which existed just a few decades ago. We are living in a modern 1990s internet era, and have not yet scratched the surface of all the speed and functionalities that blockchain technology can provide. Most likely, if you're reading this before you've begun to use the technology in your everyday life, you're still early.

Chapter 6
INTEROPERABILITY AND ORACLES

This chapter is all about communication. First, we will talk about communication between different blockchains, referred to as cross-chain communication or interoperability. Secondly, we will discuss communication between blockchains and the real world.

One of the great ironies in the current cryptocurrency landscape is that the market relies heavily on centralized entities to conduct trades. This entire thing was created to facilitate p2p transfers of value, and still here we are putting all of our trust into different exchanges that are beginning to look similar to banks. Not only do centralized exchanges defeat the purpose of cryptocurrency in itself, it is often quite inconvenient to convert between different assets. For example, let's say that Jerry holds Litecoin (LTC) on exchange A, and wants to hold Vertcoin (VTC) instead. But what if exchange A doesn't offer Vertcoin? Jerry can only purchase VTC on exchange B, and it only has a BTC to VTC pair. Now he has to sell his Litecoin into Bitcoin on exchange A, then sign up for an account at exchange B, transfer that Bitcoin to exchange B and finally conduct his purchase of VTC. This is just one of many possible examples, but you can see how it can be quite cumbersome to complete a transfer of two different currencies when most exchanges only support BTC or ETH trading pairs and not every currency is supported on every exchange.

At the end of chapter three, we briefly mentioned that the Lightning Network has the ability to swap a cryptocurrency into a different one without the use of a third party. This is known as an atomic swap and utilizes smart contract technology. The word atomic stems from the word atom which is the smallest amount of a thing and cannot be broken down further. In computer science it refers to something happening completely or not at all. In relation to cryptocurrency, an atomic swap is an all-or-nothing swap of different currencies between two people, without the use of an intermediary.

Before we dive into this explanation of atomic swaps and cross-chain communication any further, it is important to first understand why it is needed beyond just convenience. Those who have been in the cryptocurrency space for a couple years have seen multiple exchanges disappear with users' funds due to hacks, technical issues or deliberate fraud. For all intents and purposes, if you do not hold the private keys to your wallet, the funds are not yours. When you sign up for an exchange and deposit funds on the exchange's wallet, the funds are no longer yours. You may have the illusion of control because you are able to log into your account, trade and withdraw, but if the exchange were to ever disappear with your funds, make no mistake, you are in no place to recover your hard-earned wealth.

The case for atomic swaps is this: security, regulation-avoidance and speed. All of these factors are important for big and small holders of cryptocurrency alike. Suppose someone with $10M worth of a coin wanted to exchange it for something else. It would be crazy to risk putting that much money on an exchange. Also, buying or selling such a high amount of an asset comes with the risk of price slippage if done on the open market. Such person could also conduct an over-the-counter or OTC trade but this still entails putting a large sum of money in the hands of a custodial. What would such a person do in this case? An atomic swap. This technology allows any user to benefit from the security of completely diverting the use of a middle-man.

The cryptocurrency community is quite regulation adverse and any news of government entities attaching their laws to the market in a restrictive way can send prices spiraling downward. This is only a factor however because of centralized exchanges. Once atomic swaps and decentralized exchanges (DEXs) are user friendly for the average person, perhaps many of these issues will be resolved to some degree. Not only does this technology further decentralization, it also increases safety and speed because trades are conducted directly p2p, wallet to wallet, without the need to deposit or withdraw funds from any centralized entity. You are always in control of your wallet's private keys. This is also a much faster method to exchange different currencies because it does not require multiple conversions or movements of funds across platforms. Lastly, the fees associated with trading and withdrawals on centralized exchanges would be largely eliminated. Now, let's look into how it all works.

Atomic swaps are trustless. When we refer to something as trustless in cryptocurrency it does not mean that it cannot be trusted, but actually the opposite. Trust is not required. To make this concept more tangible, let's say that a US citizen traveled to China for vacation. He or she would have to exchange US dollars for Chinese yuan. However, in order to do so, this person would first have to place their trust in a bank to facilitate this transaction and provide them with the correct amount of yuan. With atomic swaps, we no longer have to place any trust in an exchange to conduct a safe transaction. We also do not have to trust the person that we are transacting with to uphold their end of the trade and not run away with our funds, or vice-versa.

The cryptographically secured smart contract used in an atomic swap cannot be broken, and therefore we are not relying on or placing our trust in any person or centralized entity, but simply in mathematics and coding. Atomic swaps are also whole and indivisible. There can be no partial swap. If Sandra wants to exchange 50 LTC for one BTC, the trade must be completed in one action, or not at all. These interactions are powered through the use of a Hash Timelock Contract (HTLC). It is a time bound smart contract between two parties and creates a cryptographic hash function that can only be verified between them. These smart contracts require that both parties acknowledge receipt of funds within a specific timeframe, or the entire transaction is voided and no funds are exchanged. These swaps usually occur on the LN "off-chain" but can be performed directly on-chain as well. At the moment, the usability of these contracts on-chain is somewhat convoluted for the average user without any programming knowledge. However, the use of on-chain atomic swaps will offer greater security and decentralization over traditional exchanges when they are perfected and made more user-friendly in the future.

Fun fact: The first cross-chain atomic swap performed on the Lightning Network was between Bitcoin and Litecoin, and occurred in November of 2017.

Atomic swaps are currently only supported for coins which are based on the Bitcoin protocol, (LTC, VTC, DCR, XZC, etcetera) but projects such as Komodo have allowed for BTC-based coins to also be traded between ETH and ETH-based tokens. This is known as an etomic swap and utilizes the Komodo platform to facilitate the p2p trade. This protocol enables on-chain swaps and is a bit easier for the average user to utilize for trading. Swaps between BTC and BTC-based coins, to ETH and ETH-based tokens is a bit more difficult to perform than regular atomic swaps because Ethereum is not built or based on Bitcoin. ERC tokens themselves are also smart contracts which sit on the Ethereum blockchain.

The Komodo platform still allows for funds to be exchanged directly from wallet to wallet, without exposure to potential attack. However, for most of the general public, decentralized exchanges and atomic swaps are not currently at a stage which is easy-to-use just yet. Much of the cryptocurrency trading volume may continue to occur on centralized exchanges in the near future, until these solutions are significantly improved. At the moment, there are many companies working to build and release fully decentralized exchanges, which support trading between a wide range of different blockchain protocols. Once this potential is unearthed, I believe there will be a dramatic shift in how cryptocurrencies are exchanged. When decentralized exchanges take solid footing in the market and are easy-to-use, there will be no governing body or other entity that can regulate the trading and advancement of cryptocurrency.

More robust and complex solutions are being developed specifically to allow blockchains to talk to one another, as well as read external data. The two most promising of which are (in my opinion) ICON and Chainlink. Below I will provide a brief summary of each project.

Think of Apple and Android. They are the two main mobile operating systems. Apple, being a walled garden, is unable to communicate with technology outside of its ecosystem. Even with there being only two ecosystems to work around, there is still undeniable fragmentation when trying to communicate between these two operating systems. Now imagine if 20 or even 30 platforms existed. What would happen if all of them were walled gardens, each having unique qualities such that the usage of multiple platforms was common among the general population? It would be a fragmented mess. ICON looks to solve this issue by bridging all of the blockchains of the world together. While many of the current 2,000+ currencies listed on Coinmarketcap are ERC20 tokens, there are still numerous platforms and coins which run their own proprietary blockchain technology. This results in many walled ecosystems that are unable to communicate with one another. ICON's slogan is "Hyperconnect the world," and it desires to be the "Ethereum" of interoperability insomuch as it aims to be the hub of a very broad range of industries. Its goal is to be a DEX and a bridge for all blockchains and platforms from multiple sectors, by building the biggest decentralized network in the world. All transactions on the ICON DEX are facilitated through the native ICX token.

This "bridge" works by having each independent blockchain community nominate a representative to the ICON Republic. Each community then connects with the republic via their representative. Representatives can propose different policies and vote on community changes through their respective channel. To give an example of a real-world application, it essentially allows government bodies, universities, hospitals, securities, banks and private companies to interact quickly and seamlessly without the use of third parties. Loopchain is the core blockchain engine of ICONLOOP (formerly "theloop"), and is at the center of the ICON network. The building of DApps and tokens on the network is performed on a platform known as ICONest.

As a side note, another highly talked about interoperability project that is often compared to ICON is Wanchain. Wanchain is a similar project to ICON in that they both utilize cross-chain communication as well as smart contracts. However, the main focus of Wanchain is on financial markets. I like to think of Wanchain as creating a decentralized financial / stock market.

In the current state of cryptocurrency technology, smart contracts are very limited to blockchain-specific applications. They virtually have no way of interacting with external real-world data. Chainlink hopes to solve this problem through the use of an oracle network. Simply put, an oracle is a hub which collects and verifies external data, and makes it readable to smart contracts. The information includes data from bank payments, retail payments, other blockchains, market data, events data and web APIs. Chainlink is building the first ever decentralized oracle network. This will connect real-world data to smart contracts on the blockchain, and intends to expand the use of smart contracts to multiple sectors across the business world.

According to the developers, anyone with a data feed or API can connect directly to a Chainlink oracle, in exchange for LINK tokens. Chainlink smart contracts are then activated based on the data provided, and various companies can utilize them based on the needs of their own business. Chainlink is rumored to have many big partnerships including one with Swift bank. However, the development team has been notoriously tight-lipped regarding any news releases or other public communications. As of right now, the testnet is operational with a few oracles, though the mainnet has yet to be released. Nonetheless, it is still one of the most anticipated projects in the cryptocurrency community.

In the future, I think that many projects in the space which offer cross-chain communication as well as oracle networks will coexist, but it still remains to be seen which ones will be successful enough to acquire large scale adoption in the long term. New technological solutions will constantly be arising and adjusting to address the problems we have discussed such as scalability, interoperability and interaction with real-world data. All of the proposed advancements essentially seek different ways to make the use of blockchain technology beneficial to our everyday lives, and make adoption as smooth and easy as possible. The technology mentioned in this section should not be seen as separate entities. Rather, everything from smart contracts and DApps, to cross-chain communication is used in conjunction with one another to create and connect decentralized digital ecosystems.

PART THREE
ENTERING THE MARKET

Chapter 7
RISK AVOIDANCE

You want to make money, right? That is the main reason why you're reading and the reason you're curious about cryptocurrency in the first place. You may be thinking, "The technology is great and everything, but I need this to be lucrative." Well, before you learn how to grow your wealth with all this information, I would like to cover, first and foremost, how to protect your capital and encourage smart investing. The cryptocurrency space is littered with blatant scams, pump-and-dumps, and projects that overpromise and under deliver. In this section, I will cover some of the most significant issues that you'll need to avoid in this space, in order to invest safely and protect your hard-earned money. There are plenty types of pitfalls but all of them can be categorized into three main categories.

- User mistakes
- Scams
- FOMO

User Mistakes

The first mistake to avoid is losing your money through simple user error. Unfortunately, this is potentially one of the easiest ways to lose money. Cryptocurrency assets are not stocks and the exchanges that you trade on are not banks. Let me break down those two statements further because they will be an overarching theme in protecting your money. In traditional stock markets, your money is protected and insured against hacks and other security breaches. There is never a need to move your stock to a secure place. No one approaches a stock broker for a physical stock certificate and puts it in a safe, it's just unnecessary. However, in cryptocurrency markets it is very important to not leave your money sitting on an exchange. Rather, it should be stored in a personal wallet where you hold your own private keys. There are multiple types of cryptocurrency wallets such as the ones listed below.

Online wallet: Website or application which operates on the cloud, and allows funds to be accessed from multiple devices with an internet connection. You do not hold your own private keys.

Software wallet: Mobile phone or desktop application where funds are only accessible from the installation device. This allows you to hold your own private keys and is considered somewhat safer than an online wallet.

Paper wallet: A physical printed copy of your generated public and private keys. You can receive funds by having them sent to the wallet address. This is best used for the storage of coins which you do not wish to move around frequently. This is safer than both online wallets and software wallets, though less convenient. However, care should be used in not misplacing your paper wallet, as well as keeping it safe from harm such as water or fire.

Hardware wallet: Physical device with no internet connection, which securely stores the user's private keys. They are able to be connected to a computer to make online transactions, but the fact that they are offline most of the time adds to their security. Also, your private keys are never exposed to the computer directly, and a user must have physical access to the device in order to send transactions. This is the most expensive type of wallet (the others are free), but also the safest option.

The main difference between wallet security will come down to whether the wallet is a hot or cold wallet. A hot wallet refers to a wallet that is connected to the internet. This includes all online, mobile and desktop wallets. It is susceptible to hacks because your private key is either out of your control or stored locally on the machine. A cold wallet refers to a wallet that does not have connection to the internet, such as a paper wallet or a hardware wallet. The two most popular hardware wallets at this time are the Ledger Nano S and the Trezor Model T. The purchase of one of these devices should be your first step to entering the space.

Now you're probably thinking, if I lose this device, are my entire cryptocurrency savings just lost forever? No! Absolutely not. (We'll cover how this works soon.) Think of a hardware wallet as simply a key that allows you to interact with the blockchain. Cryptocurrency never actually leaves the blockchain, therefore it cannot be lost solely due to the misplacement of a hardware wallet. This is similar to using a debit card. The card allows you to spend money and make payments wherever you go, but your money itself is held at a bank, and cannot be lost simply by losing your debit card. These wallets are all just different tools, used to interact with the blockchain. In a market littered with bad actors constantly looking for a way to steal user's funds, you will sleep well at night knowing that your money is safe and secure.

All of the documentation needed to set up and operate your hardware wallet will be included with the device you choose. Nonetheless, I will briefly explain how the Ledger Nano S works as it has been my device of choice. A Ledger Nano S is tamper proof on arrival, meaning the firmware is secure against alteration and will not work if it has been misused. This is to prevent someone from buying a device, tampering with it in some way, and then returning it in hopes that the next buyer will put funds on the device that can later be stolen. Regardless of which hardware wallet you choose to use, it is always best to buy directly from the manufacturer website rather than Amazon or another reseller.

When you first get the device, it will generate a 24 word seed. Make sure it generates a completely new seed! This 24 word seed defines a collection of private keys (through cryptography), which in turn will generate a wallet address. This is the single most important thing you will want to protect when dealing with cryptocurrency. If your device is ever lost, stolen or damaged, this seed will restore all of your wallets on a new device with the balances completely intact. The beauty of a hardware wallet is that when plugged into a computer, your private key stays on the device and is never visible to the internet or even the computer itself. In other words, it is completely unhackable. Your device will always be safe when connected to a computer, even against any potential malware or spyware. The rest of the time it is offline.

With that being said, your 24 word seed is only as safe as you keep it. Write them down, carve them into a stone, or place them in a vault, but absolutely do not let them touch the internet in any respect. Do not store it on a note app on your phone, do not place it on any cloud account, do not type it in a secure word file on your computer, don't even take a picture of it. Your seed should never be digitized in any way. Keep multiple physical copies of it that will not get stolen should your home be burglarized, or burned in the event of a fire (God forbid).

Your hardware wallet can store many different currencies and your 24 word seed will restore all of your assets on a new device if need be. You will also set a pin code for accessing the wallet interface when using the device, and the entire device will reset if this is entered incorrectly three times. Your device will be safe from any physical attacks, should it be stolen or tampered with by any curious person in contact with it. Again, do not share your seed or private keys with anyone, or expose them to the internet in any way, for any reason. In the new economy, you will be acting as your own bank, and it will be your sole responsibility to protect your funds. Exchanges are for active trading and are susceptible to hacks, do not leave your money there. If you do not control the private keys to any digital asset that you hold, you simply do not own it. It can be taken from you at any time with little recourse. There is no insurance or promise of safekeeping in this field. You are your own bank. I hope that I have made that clear.

The second most common user mistake is sending assets to the wrong address. You cannot send Bitcoin to a Litecoin address. It will be lost forever and there is not a person on this planet that can help you. You cannot send Ether to a Neo address. It will be lost forever and there is not a person on this planet that can help you. You cannot send Monero to a Stellar address. It will be lost forever and there is not a person on this planet that can help you. You get the point. To be completely fair, in some cases it is possible to recover incorrect deposits if sent to an exchange wallet, though it is a very convoluted process to do so, and the exchange's support team may not be quick to respond.

Before sending anything anywhere, double and triple check the address that you are sending to. Make sure that the currencies match and that the address is correct. I used to sweat bullets at first every time I transferred money anywhere, and it took me a good five to ten minutes before I finally mustered up the courage to press the send button. After a while you will get more used to it, and can take a few quick glances at the beginning and end of the address you are sending to, just to make sure that they match up. Be safe and take your time with everything that you do. Remember, you are your own bank! You have the power to send and receive money anywhere in the world, at any time, instantly, without the permission or fees of a third party.

Scams

The second major way you can lose money in this space is with scams, and believe me, there is no shortage of them. Let me preface this by saying that some of these may seem silly, but this space is full of people who have come looking for a quick and easy path to riches. Many of them have quickly learned the hard way that it is far from that. Don't get me wrong, cryptocurrency can be an excellent way to grow wealth in the long term, but the days of making easy money are gone. There is still a lot of money to be made, but if you have entered the space because you once heard of someone buying thousands of Bitcoin for a few cents each in 2010 and are hoping to make 1,000x gains in a few months, it is unlikely. This is not a get-rich-quick scheme, and there are unfortunately many traps to avoid when investing in this space. With that being said, here are some of the most common scams and how to avoid them.

Impersonators

The most common form of impersonators are those found on Twitter. Follow any well-recognized person in the cryptocurrency space and you are guaranteed to see a user underneath their posts pretending to be them. They will often have a very similar handle with a letter or two changed. Their profile picture, banner and bio will be the same and the overall profile will be somewhat convincing to the untrained eye. Under the post of the legitimate user, they will advertise a giveaway and promise that those who enter will receive free Ether. All you have to do to enter is send a certain amount of Ether to their wallet address. In the real-world this would be similar to saying, "Send me five dollars and I will send you back 50." But alas, the euphoria of the "get-rich-quick" mentality in this space has led many to fall for this blatant deception. This issue has gotten so rampant that many popular figures in the crypto-world have gone so far as to include the phrase "Not Giving Away ETH" in their username. In many cases, the scam-bots have ridiculously copied this information to their own profile, and have continued to attempt to scam people.

Similar to Twitter profile impersonators, impersonators also exist within the ICO space and elsewhere. This may appear in the form of users pretending to be team members on Twitter, in Telegram groups, on Facebook pages, or on Reddit. I have even received messages sent from official email addresses that have been taken over. The hacker will send out emails appearing to be urgent, asking people to send money to their wallet address. This is rare, but it can happen. These attempts usually raise an eyebrow though as they often include some sort of second chance, early sale, huge bonus, or other tactic that would pressure users into sending funds quickly, without first thinking. If you ever feel rushed to send money somewhere, don't. Always take your time and be sure of what you are doing.

Questionable ICOs

When you begin your research, whether it be an ICO or an existing coin, you will sometimes stop and think, "Why does this project need a token to operate its business?" You would be completely justified in thinking that. A lot of the projects in this space are unnecessary, vaporware, or do not require tokenization to operate. The other half are blatant scams. Bundle that in with teams which often overpromise and underdeliver, and you may soon realize that finding a good project in this space is similar to finding a gem in a field of mud.

When you do find that gem though, you will be glad you took the time to do your research. Do not buy anything just because someone on Youtube, Twitter or Reddit says to. It may very well be a good project that turns out to make many people rich, or it could be a huge scam that you lose money on. More often than not, it is the latter. In either scenario, you are completely in charge and responsible for where you put your money. My purpose is not to tell you what to invest in, but rather to provide you with the knowledge and forewarning on how to navigate this space effectively.

Phishing

I have seen entire websites perfectly cloned numerous times. Not just in the ICO space, but even with exchanges and wallet interfaces such as Myetherwallet. Myetherwallet is one of the most popular and trusted interfaces used to store Ether and ERC tokens. I have seen this website replicated to a tee, with one of the letters in the url having a barely visible accent or other small nuance. Be sure to always double-check that the url you are visiting is correct, and bookmark any frequently visited ones so there is no chance of confusion. (However, this is not a problem if you have a hardware wallet such as a Ledger or Trezor!)

Also, many trusted exchanges such as Binance or even Coinbase have had their website cloned, in an attempt to have users enter their login information. Always be sure to activate 2FA or two-factor authorization when logging into any service which stores your cryptocurrency. This links your account to the Google authorization app on your smartphone, and is only accessible via the local device. A new 6-digit authentication code is generated every 30 seconds for all of the accounts linked to your device. Enabling 2FA will lock access to your account without entering the code. Any potential hacker would not only need login information, but also physical access to your smartphone.

Cloud-Based Mining

There are a couple services on the internet that allow you to buy mining power and mine cryptocurrency without a physical machine. I will keep this one simple. Do not pay for any service that wants you to sign a contract or invest in a Bitcoin mining center. This does not make sense from a business perspective. In order for you to make a positive ROI, you would have to make more money mining than the cost which you initially spent. If a company takes in less money than the profit they are providing you, they are losing money. If they could produce more money mining themselves and keeping the coin, they would simply mine themselves and keep their profit. There is also very little proof of legitimacy behind these services. No one is giving away money.

Pyramid or Ponzi Schemes

You may have seen a meme going around of a man named Carlos Matos screaming "BITCONNECT" while parading around on stage. If you haven't, search the word Bitconnect on Youtube. This is hands down the most infamous ponzi scheme in the crypto-space. In essence, it was a platform which promised around a 1% daily gain on your money based on profits from an automated trading bot. The platform accepted Bitcoin in exchange for a now worthless Bitconnect token. Long story short, the trading bot never existed and all of the "profit" was paid out based on new users signing up under the old ones. This structure of multi-level marketing AKA pyramid scheme eventually collapsed when they ran out of new users signing up to pay the existing users. There are many horror stories of people losing their life savings through this platform, even though many outspoken figures in the crypto-space had been warning people day in and day out. Anything that promises a guaranteed return on investment is lying to you. If you take away one lesson from this, be careful and use common sense when investing and moving money.

Fear of Missing Out

As the best friend of greed, FOMO or the fear of missing out is by far the most tempting way to lose money when investing in cryptocurrency. In a major bull market, you will witness price movements that you never thought possible. You will miss opportunities to make six-figures in the span of a few days, multiple times per week. It will be a gut-wrenching experience to watch opportunity after opportunity slip away. You won't catch every rocket and the ones which you do, many times you will sell too early. This is the reality of trading. However, I beg of you, do not buy into the top of a coin that has pumped 80% in a day or one which has pumped 1,000% in two weeks. If you ever decide to buy something only because it is listed as one of the top gainers for the day, don't.

The fear of missing out on massive price movements is very real, and it is often very tempting to buy into something which seems to be heading upward in a straight line, with the expectation that it will never fall. Spoiler, it will, and downward price corrections can happen just as quickly as upward movements. You should be researching and entering projects which you want to have in your portfolio long before they have a massive price increase, not during. It is easy to enter today's winner, many people do it and put money into the pockets of those who have done their research beforehand and are now waiting to exit on the ride up. On the other hand, finding and entering tomorrow's winner is where you will see the greatest benefit. Do not lose hope in moving at your own pace when finding and entering the right coins, these opportunities will come around time and time again. I wish I could tell you step-by-step what to look for, when to get in, and when to get out, but I would have retired by now. My hope is that this chapter has instilled in you a focus to protect your capital and think critically. It will save you a lot of money in the long run. In these fast moving markets, trade slowly, trade carefully and trade deliberately.

Fun fact: A massive price movement can also be the result of an underhanded ploy known as a pump-and-dump. A pump-and-dump (P&D) happens when a group of people coordinate to artificially inflate the price of a cryptocurrency through order book manipulation and public FOMO. One of the most infamous schemes of this malicious tactic was performed on a coin named Chaincoin (CHC). Youtubers and other crypto-influencers shamelessly proclaimed to their followers that the masternode rewards from this coin would grant them passive income for life, if the coin reached a price level of $100. However, these people had already accumulated the coin privately and were only boosting the price in an attempt to sell to unsuspecting victims. In 2017 from June 24 to July 14, the coin went from a low of six cents to a high of over six dollars, representing a 100x return over 20 days (before quickly tumbling back down).

Chapter 8
MARKET TRENDS AND TECHNICAL ANALYSIS

I should premise this chapter by saying that technical analysis (TA) in itself deserves an entire book, of which many exist. Technical analysis and market trends are not unique to cryptocurrency markets. However, there are some differences to be aware of that differentiate crypto-markets from legacy markets. The main things we will cover in this chapter are BTC dominance and its effect on the market as well as coin supply and how it skews the perspective of value, along with a few other price indicators.

As you may have heard before, markets move in cycles. One of the biggest things to consider when investing in cryptocurrency markets is BTC dominance; specifically if it is in an uptrend or a downtrend. This basically means, of the total crypto market-cap, what percentage of that value is Bitcoin, and in general, where is the money moving? The market cap of any coin is its price multiplied by supply. For example, a coin with a supply of 10 million and a price of $10 would have a market capitalization of $100 million. Since everything in the market is currently priced in Satoshi (0.00000001 Bitcoin), when the price of Bitcoin moves, the price of everything else moves as well. Note that a Satoshi is one hundred millionth of a Bitcoin, similar to how a penny is one hundredth of a dollar; this is the smallest denomination of a Bitcoin. This means that if Bitcoin moves up or down in price, an altcoin will be affected in one of five ways.

If Bitcoin moves up in price.

An altcoin will remain at the same USD price and lose Satoshi value if the percentage gain in Bitcoin is equal to the percentage loss in Satoshi. Secondly, an altcoin can go down in both Satoshi value and USD value if the percentage loss in Satoshi is greater than the percentage gain in Bitcoin. Third, an altcoin can gain USD value but lose Satoshi value if the percentage increase in Bitcoin is greater than the percentage decrease in Satoshi. Fourth, a coin can move up in both USD and Satoshi value. Lastly, an altcoin can remain at the same Satoshi value and increase in USD value based on the BTC price movement.

If Bitcoin moves down in price.

Inversely, if Bitcoin drops in price then an altcoin still has five options. First, it can stay the same price in USD but gain Satoshi value if the percentage rise in Satoshi is equal to the percentage loss in Bitcoin. Secondly, it can gain Satoshi value and USD value if the percentage gain in Satoshi is greater than the percentage loss of Bitcoin. Third, an altcoin can lose USD value but gain Satoshi value if the percentage decrease in Bitcoin is greater than the percentage increase in Satoshi. Fourth, it can drop in both USD value and Satoshi value. Lastly, an altcoin can remain at the same Satoshi value and lose USD value based on the BTC price movement.

This may seem quite confusing at first, but once you begin to trade and read the order books it will start to make more sense. Just remember that the underlying value of most altcoins are priced in Satoshi, so a change in Bitcoin's value can have a big impact on the market.

The Blockchain Revolution

A lot of coins also have an ETH pairing as well, so take into consideration Ethereum's price the same as you would Bitcoin's price if you plan on trading into altcoins with Ether.

Here is a quick example to solidify these concepts. Let's say that Bitcoin is priced at $10,000. An altcoin is worth 50,000 Satoshi (0.00050000 Bitcoin), or in other words $5. The next day Bitcoin has a 10% gain and is now worth $11,000. This coin's price action can move in 5 different ways. First, it could remain the same in USD at $5 ($4.95) but take a 10% loss in Satoshi. It is now worth only 45,000 Satoshi (0.00045000 Bitcoin). (Side note: these numbers are approximate because it takes a greater % gain to offset a % loss. For example, a 10% loss on $100 is now $90. However, a 10% gain on $90 is only $99.) Second, this same coin could suffer a 20% loss in Satoshi and drop to 40,000 Satoshi (0.00040000 Bitcoin). Its price is now negative in USD value and Satoshi value because its loss in Satoshi was greater than Bitcoin's gain. It currently sits at $4.40.

However, this altcoin could take only a 5% loss in Satoshi and still be positive USD because of the rise in Bitcoin. In this case it sits at 47,500 Satoshi (0.00047500 Bitcoin), but is offset by the gain in Bitcoin so its price is positive in USD at $5.23. Fourth, it could have a Satoshi gain as well as a Bitcoin gain. Let's say the Satoshi value doesn't drop but instead moves up 10% to 55,000 Sats (0.00055000 Bitcoin). Its price is now $6.00 ($6.05) instead of $5.50 because its Satoshi gain is stacked on top of the underlying gain in Bitcoin. Lastly, this coin could simply remain the same in Satoshi value at 50,000 (0.00050000 Bitcoin), and take a USD bump up to $5.50 because of the gain in Bitcoin.

It is of the utmost importance that you look not only at USD value but also the Satoshi amount when trading and also when monitoring your portfolio. As we have just seen in some cases, you could be seeing a steady or even increasing value in USD but be losing Satoshi value at the same time. This type of price action can also have the effect of making Satoshi losses look less significant than they are, because of the gain in the price of Bitcoin. In many of these cases, it would have been better just to hold Bitcoin, the underlying asset itself, rather than trading it for an altcoin. This works the same with Ethereum or any other large-cap coin that is a common trading pair between other altcoins.

Bitcoin dominance refers to Bitcoin's market capitalization in reference to the combined market cap of everything else in the crypto-market. In general, when Bitcoin dominance is in an uptrend, it is safer to hold Bitcoin because that is where money is moving (altcoins are losing Satoshi value). When Bitcoin dominance is falling, it is usually better to hold altcoins because that is where the money is moving (altcoins are gaining Satoshi value). Of course, it is nearly impossible to time the market and predict when these trends will reverse in one direction or the other, but it is important to understand that these trends exist and to move with the market, not against it. As a rule of thumb, if Bitcoin dominance is increasing, it is best to convert at least some of your holdings into Bitcoin. Inversely, when Bitcoin dominance is falling, it is usually best to sell some of your Bitcoin into some of the altcoins that you have researched and have on your watchlist. This will vary of course, based on market sentiment and news surrounding the coin you are holding. Some coins can move against this trend based on the current news or hype surrounding it. In any case, be aware of which way the market is moving.

Predicting the timing of these shifts is tricky because there is no concrete rule which indicates a shift. In my experience from observation, if the price of Bitcoin is steady or moving up moderately, altcoins will tend to move up with it at the same or a higher pace. If the price of Bitcoin shoots up very quickly, the market capitalization of altcoins tends to dip in favor of the anticipated gains from holding Bitcoin. When a new wave of money first enters the market, it will initially go to Bitcoin and then trickle down into Ethereum and the rest of the altcoins as people discover them.

There is a lot of talk within the community of when the price action of altcoins will be decoupled from BTC movements, but in order to reach that point, every coin must be able to be purchased directly with USD and other fiat currencies. Even then, I think that the price of Bitcoin will still act as an index for the overall market sentiment and price action. Also, if this scenario were to unfold, it still presents even greater problems as it would require a high level of regulation and centralization, the antithesis of decentralization and "the people's money." A USD or other fiat pairing for every coin would defeat the very purpose which crypto tries to push forward. For the foreseeable future, Bitcoin will have a huge effect on the market and you must be aware of which direction its market-cap dominance is moving in order to trade effectively. There will be coins which contradict the market trends and move against what the overall market is doing based on technological releases, good or bad news, quality of the project, public sentiment, exchange listings etcetera but the direction of Bitcoin dominance should always serve as a reference for which to base where you allocate the wealth in your portfolio.

To dive into this a bit more, the linkage of Bitcoin and altcoins is seen by many people in the crypto-community as a massive hindrance to overall market growth and maturity. The price binding of Bitcoin to altcoins in the crypto market is akin to Amazon having control over the entire stock market. Imagine if every stock worldwide were priced in denominations of Amazon stock. If Amazon dropped by 10%, everything else would most likely tumble as well. This is the cryptocurrency market in its current form. To combat this, there are some coins in the crypto-market known as stablecoins, which are tied in price to fiat currencies. The most widely used at this moment is Tether (USDT), which is tied to the USD. Tether is issued by Tether Limited and is supposedly backed one-to-one by actual USD. However, there is a lot of skepticism within the crypto-community on this statement because these records have not been audited. (I will allow you to find the irony here.) Other stablecoins have also been tied to the USD such as TrueUSD (TUSD) and GeminiDollar (GUSD), with more expected to be introduced by various institutions in the future.

Another common blunder that all new players should be aware of when entering the crypto-space is not looking at supply. A cheap cryptocurrency in terms of USD does not mean that it is actually cheap or has a high growth potential. For example, if a coin has a price of $0.10 it may seem cheap, but if the supply is 1 billion then it already has a market cap of $100 million. On the other hand, if a coin is priced at $10 (100x more expensive) but its supply is only 5 million, then its market cap is $50 million. With the fundamentals, team quality and magnitude of the project all being equal, based on these metrics alone, the $10 coin is actually "cheaper" and has a higher potential return on investment (ROI) because its market cap has twice as much room to grow. Try not to focus so much on the dollar value of a coin but rather its market cap. With that being said, many of the "cheap" coins have made insane returns for the very reason that people see it as a cheap entry into the market, without taking into consideration its supply and overall market cap. For example, many veterans in the space predicted that XRP, with a supply at the time of over 39 billion coins, would never hit a dollar. Surprise, surprise, it skyrocketed to well over $3 before correcting back down in the crash of early 2018.

The psychological lure of buying cheap coins has been lucrative in the past as a rush of new investors entered the market with limited experience. This trend may very will continue for a while longer in the future, though in my humble opinion, as time goes on the easy money will start to disappear. With that being said, many illogical things happen in a cryptocurrency bull market and I could very well be wrong, so take this analysis with a grain of salt.

Next, we have demand. I'm sure everyone has heard the phrase "supply and demand" at some point during their lives. This concept drives price action in traditional markets and it also drives price movement within crypto-markets. The supply of a coin will influence its price, but two projects with a similar supply can have vastly different prices. What is the difference? Demand. The top 30 coins as I'm writing this all have something special going for them. A lot of them are platforms such as Ethereum, EOS, Stellar, Neo, ICON, etc that have their own blockchains. The tokens that sit on these platforms do not reach as high of a market cap as the platform itself because they only represent a niche market. The infrastructure itself is what attracts large volume and interest from others wanting to build on top of it. These sorts of projects are often more "safe" from volatility, and have better long term success than the niche projects which are built on top of their blockchains. An ERC20 token will never have a higher market cap than Ethereum itself and a NEP-5 token will never have a higher market cap than Neo itself.

Coins such as Monero or Dash have privacy features built in, meaning that you can move value across the blockchain without the amount being publicly visible, or having the wallet address be traceable back to you or anyone else. These coins also run their own individual blockchains rather than sitting on a platform. Projects such as Nano (formerly Raiblocks) have fast speeds and little to no transaction fees. Still other projects have first-mover advantage and are supported by active developers who have managed to keep relevance in the competitive market. Various other coins have gained their rank simply by the backing of big institutions.

All of these factors and unique intricacies play a role in a coin's demand. The scrutiny of these factors can also be referred to as fundamental analysis (FA), and should be considered when analyzing expected growth potential and ROI. For example, it is useful to compare new platforms to existing ones, compare new exchange tokens to existing ones, compare new privacy coins to existing ones and compare coins with unique scaling solutions to the technology of top existing solutions. See where the market cap of the top coins in a category are, and compare it to the underdog in the same category that has not yet reached its full potential.

Trends with Volume

As we mentioned earlier, volume is one of the biggest indicators for long term price stability. A higher market-cap correlates with higher volume as a coin gains more recognition and interest. It is harder to manipulate the price in either direction for coins which have high volume. This is why Bitcoin is usually much less volatile than the altcoins. Its high volume makes it difficult for anyone to sway the order books unless they have a massive amount of buying or selling power. Large buy orders will be eaten up by sellers without pushing up the price, and large sell orders will be eaten up by the buyers without pushing down the price.

Analyzing volume can also be a valuable market indicator for price action. This can be looked at in timeframes as short as a few hours or as long as a few days or weeks. Below I will outline a few price signals based on volume and the market mentality behind these movements. As a disclaimer, technical analysis should not be used as a definitive signal for price movement in any direction, but rather as a tool to analyze weighted probabilities and make an informed decision.

Volume increasing + price rising = Bullish

A rising price and a rising volume may indicate that there are more buyers than sellers in the market, and that the buying pressure is increasing. The price may continue its uptrend in the near term.

Volume decreasing + price falling = Bullish

A falling price and decreasing volume may indicate that selling pressure is running thin. The price may be due for an upward movement in the near term.

Volume increasing + price falling = Bearish

A falling price and increasing volume may indicate that there are more sellers than buyers in the market, and that the selling pressure is increasing. The price may be due for further downward movement in the near term.

Volume decreasing + price rising = Bearish

A rising price and decreasing volume may indicate that buying pressure is beginning to dry up. The upward price movement may be unsustainable and could be due for a downward movement in the near term.

Using volume as a price indicator can be very versatile for any timeframe that you are trying to identify a trend for. It can be used to analyze segments of time as short as a few hours, or as long as a few weeks or months, to identify larger price trends.

Fun fact: The exact origin of the terms "Bull" and "Bear" used to describe market movement is unknown, though many speculate that it correlates with how each animal attacks. Bulls slash upward with their horns, while bears slash downward with their claws.

Reading Candlesticks

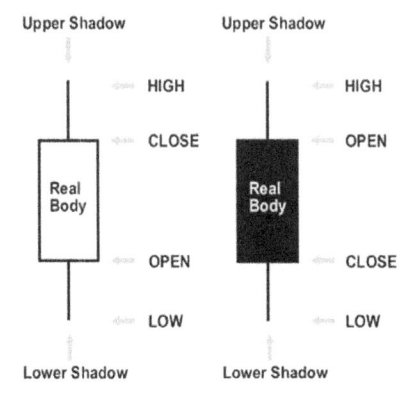

A candle is a visual representation of price movement over a period of time. They appear on price graphs and can be as short as five minutes or even as long as days, weeks or months. A candle which represents 15 minutes of price movement would be referred to as a 15 minute candle. Similarly, a candle which represents an hour, a day or even a month of price movement would be considered an hourly candle, a daily candle or a monthly candle respectively. Candles can be green or red depending on which way the price moves in a period time, with green representing upward movement and red representing downward movement. If a candle is green, the candle which forms after it will begin forming at the top of the body of the previous candle, also referred to as the closing price. If a candle is red, the candle which forms after it will begin forming at the bottom of the body of the previous candle. In this case, the bottom of the body of a red candle is its closing price. Candles also have wicks, sometimes referred to as shadows. These are lines which indicate the highs and lows within the candle's timeframe.

Support and Resistance

Often times when looking at price graphs on both short and long timeframes, you are able to draw lines that connect certain price trends. These can either be two parallel lines or two lines which intersect to form a triangle. These lines are completely straight and should not have any bends or curves. The bottom line acts as a price support and connects the local low price points in a trend. The top line acts as a price resistance and connects the local high points in a trend. If the price drops below the bottom line we refer to it as breaking support. This may indicate bearish price action in the near term. However, if the price breaks above the upper resistance line, bullish price action can be expected in the near term. If a support line is broken it can often turn into a line of resistance. Vice versa, if a resistance line is broken it can often turn into a line of support. *Tradingview.com* allows users to chart almost any traditional stock or digital asset in real time. You can practice drawing your own support and resistance lines for almost anything that you're interested in trading.

Charting patterns

Here we will go over a few of the most common patterns to look for when analyzing a price chart. With this knowledge you will be able to spot fundamental price signals and interpret their meaning effectively. These are very powerful indicators and should provide you with a strong foundation to future technical analysis.

Rising Wedge

A rising wedge is indicated by higher highs and higher lows. It forms an upward pointing triangle shape that is observed based on the support and resistance lines drawn within a certain timeframe. A rising wedge is a bearish pattern because it is usually followed by a downward price movement near the tip of the triangle. This pattern typically occurs after a drop in price, and is therefore referred to as a continuation pattern. Opposingly, if it occurs after an upward movement in price, it is then considered a reversal pattern.

Falling Wedge

A falling wedge is indicated by lower highs and lower lows. It forms a downward pointing triangle shape that is observed based on the support and resistance lines drawn within a certain timeframe. A falling wedge is a bullish pattern because it is usually followed by an upward price movement near the tip of the triangle. This pattern typically occurs after a rise in price, and is therefore referred to as a continuation pattern. Opposingly, if it occurs after a downward movement in price, is then considered a reversal pattern.

Ascending Triangle

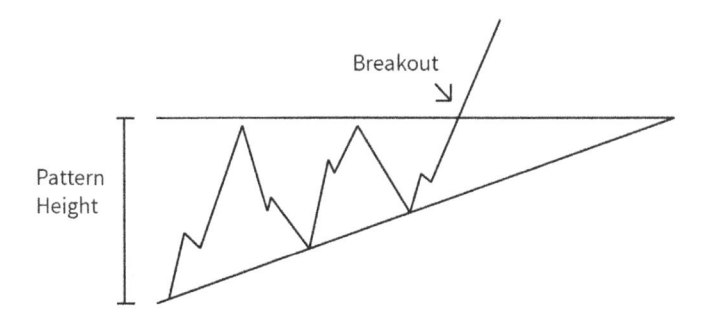

The ascending triangle pattern is indicated by higher lows and equal highs which are unable to break resistance. This can sometimes look visually similar to a rising wedge, though there are two key differences. Instead of the resistance line trending upward, it is flat. Also, an ascending triangle is a bullish pattern, opposed to a rising wedge which is bearish.

Descending Triangle

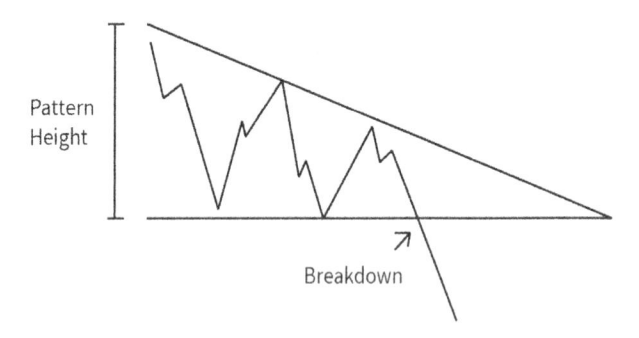

The descending triangle pattern is indicated by lower highs and equal lows which bounce off of support. This can sometimes look visually similar to a falling wedge, though there are two key differences. Instead of the support line trending downward, it is flat. Also, a descending triangle is a bearish pattern, opposed to a falling wedge which is bullish.

Head & Shoulders

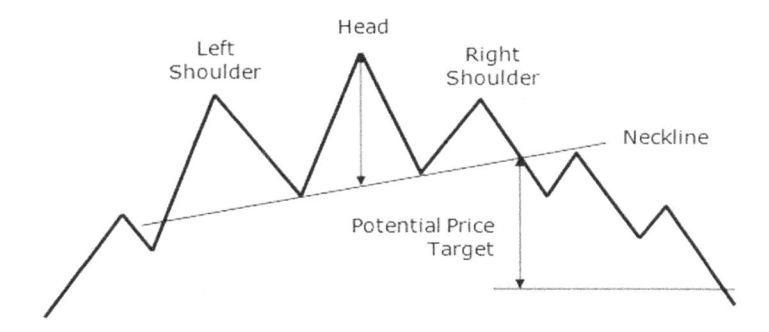

A head and shoulders pattern is indicated by three critical price movements. It begins with a local high, followed by another higher local high, and is finally completed by a third lower local high. (This usually looks more like a mountainscape than an actual "head and shoulders" when depicted visually on a price graph.) This pattern will typically occur after an uptrend and is a bearish reversal pattern. The bottom of the right shoulder is usually followed by more downward price movement.

An inverse head and shoulders, similar to what it sounds, is this same pattern flipped upside down. It is a bullish reversal pattern and indicates further upward price movement at the top of the right shoulder.

It is important to remember that all of these patterns are only indicators based on market mentality. They can sometimes fail, can be interpreted differently by various people and scenarios, and should not be viewed as guarantees to any future price movements when interpreting a chart.

As a final tip, do not trade according to what the media releases. They will always lose you money. There was recently a chart released by Twitter user Jacob

Canfield, otherwise known as "IloveCrypto," which plotted the timing of bullish and bearish tweets released by the CNBC Fast Money account against the historic price movements of BTC. Unsurprisingly, they were bullish at every local top and bearish at every local bottom. It was the perfect reflection of an amateur trader's mindset. They were essentially feeding their followers the perfect times to buy high and sell low. It is often times very profitable to take a contrarian approach when analyzing what any news outlet is calling for in terms of price direction. In other words, when you see the media calling for a huge rally in prices, begin to take profit and exit the market. When the narrative is all doom and gloom, this is your best entrance.

Chapter 9
DYOR AND BEGIN TRADING

Here I will break down the process that I use, step by step, to find, research and determine potential coins that I want to invest in. Then I will explain step by step how to actually buy and store any particular cryptocurrency. I would like to reiterate that this is not financial advice and I am not a financial advisor. This is simply my personal methodology for finding viable projects with growth potential in the cryptocurrency space.

Discovery

Regardless of if you are looking to enter an existing coin or an ICO, the first step is to hear about it. You can't begin to research something if you don't know it exists yet. So how do you find new projects? For ICOs this is as simple as visiting an ICO calendar website such as *coinschedule.com* or *tokenmarket.net*. (There is a full list of websites which provide ICO calendars and ratings at the end of the book under resources.) From what I have seen thus far, the higher-cap coins are usually blockchain platforms and protocols themselves, not the DApps or tokens for niche markets. The latter is built upon the former, not the other way around. To give a more concrete example, many websites on the internet will fail, but the internet itself will never go away. The infrastructure will always remain, so invest in that.

As a disclaimer, ICO investing can be somewhat riskier than buying existing coins because of all the projects which again, tend to overpromise and underdeliver. On the other hand, if you do find a stellar project and the token metrics make for a small market cap, it can offer substantially higher ROI potential. The website you visit will have detailed instructions on how to sign-up for and participate in the token sale.

If you are looking for an already existing coin, your one-stop-shop is *coinmarketcap.com*. This is the hub of all things cryptocurrency and is probably the most useful and most visited crypto-related website. It has almost every coin in existence listed with links to their website, Telegram group, Twitter, and Reddit. Coinmarketcap also has historic price graphs for every coin with charts of the USD price alongside the Satoshi price. They also list the exchanges that a certain coin can be purchased on, along with pairing and volume information. CMC lists the gainers and losers of the day, and this can also be sorted by the hour or even week. You can view historic graphs of BTC dominance as well as historic graphs of the overall market-cap and the altcoin market-cap. It can be overwhelming at first but should make a lot more sense once you start looking around the website for a few minutes.

Fun fact: There are archives of Coinmarketcap dating back to 2013 so you can see how much money you could have made, had you known about this a few years ago. This information can be found in a subsection under tools named historical snapshots.

Next, start looking around. Yes, this sounds like a lot of work. There are over 2,000 cryptocurrencies listed on Coinmarketcap and most of them will fail. Finding a good project in the cryptocurrency-space involves you digging through the mud for a diamond. Once you familiarize yourself with this space, it is very easy to spot what the mud looks like and differentiate it from the diamonds. There are 100 coins listed per page and I personally recommend staying on page 1-2, maybe 3 if you're feeling adventurous. The further down you go, the higher the potential ROI if you find something that does happen to be an extremely overlooked and undervalued project, but your risk increases exponentially after about the third page. Again, just my humble opinion. You should be spending no more than 2-3 minutes on a website before coming to your own conclusion on if it is worth investigating further.

There are other sources to find good projects, without checking every single website on Coinmarketcap, such as Twitter, Reddit and Youtube. Just search "crypto" or "cryptocurrency" on any of the platforms mentioned and you've opened pandora's box. Finding one good project can also lead to finding other promising related ones, as people on these platforms will mention various things which they have faith in. Now, it is time to do your own research.

By far one of the most famously used acronyms in crypto is DYOR. It stands for "do your own research." This is not skimming through a list on Coinmarketcap or watching a Youtube video on the top coins of the month. This happens when you find something worth your time, and again, once you familiarize yourself with the space and filter out all the noise, it is very easy to see what is worth investigating beyond three minutes. Once you have found this project which stands out to you, it's time to research.

I usually start by visiting the website of a coin that I'm interested in and reading the whitepaper. After you read the whitepaper, be sure to analyze the team members. Visit their LinkedIn profiles, and maybe even do a google search on them. Have they worked on any blockchain projects before? Were they successful? What is their job history? After reading the whitepaper and researching the team, I then categorize the coin as something. What does it do? Is it a platform? Does it serve a broad range of people or industries? Does it solve scalability in a unique way? Does it have masternodes? Does it have private transaction capabilities or smart contracts? What is the main incentive to hold the coin that will influence its price? Does it have staking rewards? Where is it based? How is their marketing? What is on their roadmap?

This can all be done mentally, but just ask yourself these sorts of questions. Ask yourself questions on the types of problems the project solves and how well it solves them. Look at the price and supply and where it currently sits on its historic price graph. Is it close to the all-time high or has it had a recent pullback? Find out why. Find out everything you can from multiple sources.

Almost every community has a dedicated chatroom on Telegram. Join it and ask questions. Reach out to the community admins in the chatroom and ask them questions. Another tactic I like to employ is searching for the ticker symbol on Twitter. There is a big community of cryptocurrency enthusiasts on Twitter, and while it is important to take their advice with a grain of salt, their insights can sometimes be helpful in finding out information about certain projects. Also, when searching for community opinions and sentiment on any coin, be sure to use "-filter:links" after the ticker symbol that you are searching. Twitter is rampant with bots that spam referral links to exchanges and tag a plethora of different coins in order to show up in searches. This can make it difficult to find what you are looking for. A cash tag search should look something like this: "$btc -filter:links" or "$eth -filter:links."

You can also use Reddit to see what other people are saying about the coin you are researching. The dedicated Reddit page for any particular coin can be found via its listing on Coinmarketcap. If someone presents a fact that you are unsure about, search for it and see if it is confirmed or denied by other sources. Watch some videos on Youtube, but be sure to verify the information that is being fed. Gather bits and pieces of information from multiple sources without being swayed one way or another too heavily by any one source. Form your own opinions, then create a list of coins that you think look promising.

I am very bullish on Chinese projects in general. There is a lot of FUD (fear uncertainty and doubt) going around that China is banning crypto, but I think they are actually going to be a main powerhouse in the space. Take a guess at who holds the most blockchain patents globally? You may be surprised to know that it is the Chinese central bank. That's right, and the second highest is Alibaba, China's biggest online marketplace. Projects such as VeChain, Waltonchain, Ontology, Zilliqa, High Performance Blockchain, CPChain, and Neo all have roots in China. Some of these projects even have connections to banks as well as government institutions.

In general, if a project is from an Asian country, especially China, Korea or Singapore, I like to dig deeper into it. Other characteristics I like to look for include real-world applications, support from big institutions, partnerships or connections to other tokens, and incentives for token holders such as staking capabilities. This is not all encompassing, but my point is to identify things that set a cryptocurrency apart from the rest of the sea. Identify recognition and community support. Identify a strong team, strong fundamentals and value.

As a side note to your research, you may find many projects which proclaim they have a partnership with another coin or other entity such as a large business. Be aware of the implications this has as it is often very misleading and vague. One common type of "partnership" that is mentioned in the cryptocurrency-space is known as a MOU or memorandum of understanding. This is simply a gentleman's agreement to collaborate in the future. A memorandum of understanding is different from a strategic partnership, which involves a legally binding contract, and typically entails at least one party investing in the other.

It is important to not put all of your eggs in one basket, while also not spreading yourself too thin. I rather take the time to deeply research a solid 3-5 projects, than to enter 10-15 just for the sake of diversification. Everyone has different risk tolerances and you have to decide for yourself what you're comfortable with. There is nothing intrinsically wrong with being in 10-15 coins if you find that all of them have potential. Diversification also has the benefit of allowing you to roll profits from coins which have shot up in price, to those which have not yet risen. However, you should be careful with this strategy and know when to simply hold on to profit rather than reinvesting it.

Entering the Market

There is no lack of crypto-to-crypto exchanges. Once you're in, you're in. The hardest part is getting your first coin. Now that you know what you want to invest in, it's time to turn the fiat money sitting in your bank account into digital currency on the blockchain. There are a couple ways to do this, but the easiest and most convenient by far is through Coinbase. Another traditional crypto-to-crypto exchange that has recently allowed USD markets is Bittrex. The third entrance that I know of, which is relatively simple, is Abra Global. With all of these services, it should be as straightforward as signing up and linking your bank account, but in some cases these exchanges may require KYC or know your customer restrictions. Once you are approved, most fiat-to-crypto exchanges have BTC, ETH and LTC markets as standard, with support being added for more coins as time goes on.

I should mention that Coinbase Pro (formerly GDAX) has the most robust price charting capabilities for USD markets. Their market page allows you to set limit orders which execute when a certain price is met, rather than simply buying in or selling at the current price. Your Coinbase account is automatically linked to Coinbase Pro (this is free), and the desktop platform will give you greater functionality when trading, compared to simply using the mobile app.

Once you have completed your first purchase of BTC or ETH, you can store it in a hardware wallet if you are satisfied with what you have and do not wish to buy anything else. (This will be explained in more detail soon.) However, if you would like to purchase a coin that does not have a USD or other fiat pairing, the process is as follows. In order to buy a specific coin that you have been looking at, go to the markets tab on Coinmarketcap for that coin. This should show the exchanges that it is listed on as well as the price and volume for BTC and ETH pairs respectively. Head to an exchange that it is listed on and sign up for it. Try to pick the exchange and trading pair with the highest volume as it will be easier to buy and sell into a liquid market.

If you are picking respectable projects, the most common exchanges at this time are Binance and Bittrex. Some lesser known but still legitimate coins may be available on Bibox, Huobi, OKEx or Kucoin. I tend to stay away from coins on smaller exchanges for two reasons. The credibility of the project and the safety of the exchange. If a project has any merit, it is usually listed on at least one of these six exchanges. However, in some cases if you just happen to be early on finding a gem, it may not have been listed yet. There is still a lot of money to be made on more obscure exchanges so use your best judgement on where to buy certain coins. Explore and find out what your risk tolerance is. As a final note, new exchanges will always be arising and by the time you enter the market, there may be a few new trustworthy exchanges (or decentralized exchanges) that have not been mentioned here.

The next step is to send your BTC or ETH from the wallet that you bought it from with fiat, to the exchange wallet of your choice. Do this by first finding the wallet address for the exchange wallet that you will be sending to. You can copy and paste this address, or scan a QR code if sending from your mobile phone. This should make more sense once you begin using these exchanges and can visualize the process. Proceed to send the transaction and wait for it to confirm. You can view the status of your transaction by viewing the block explorer for the specific coin you are transacting with. The block explorer for Bitcoin can be found at *blockchain.com/explorer* and the block explorer for Ethereum can be found at *etherscan.io*. You can find your transaction status by searching using your transaction id or the wallet address which you sent funds to. Once it is confirmed by the exchange, you are ready to trade.

From here, navigate to the market for which you would like to trade in and familiarize yourself with the orderbook and how it works. Interpret the price graph and play around with the five minute, 15 minute, and hour candles, to see where the price was, where it is now, and where it might be headed. Remember, you do not immediately have to buy in to something. You can wait a few hours or even days if you think the price is headed down in the short term. If you think the price is headed up soon it may be smarter to buy in at the moment. Also, you can average-in starting with 25% and complete your position over the course of a few days or even weeks, depending on how the chart looks. Check both the historic charts on Coinmarketcap to see where the price is overall, as well as the chart on the exchange order book.

Then, when you are comfortable with your plan, set your buy order somewhat below the highest bidder and wait for it to be filled. If the current price is significantly too high for your comfort level and you expect it to come down within a few hours or days, you can set it significantly below the current price. If the price is in a good range within your comfort level, you can still set it slightly below the current price and wait for it to be filled to get a better deal. In either case, if you are setting a limit order below the current market price, whether it be slightly below or significantly below, walk away from the computer. Do not stare at the screen for hours waiting for it to fill. You will end up buying higher. Many exchanges have trading-bots running that will outbid you by a few Satoshi, and you will end up moving your order higher and higher out of frustration. Walk away, it will eventually fill.

This method works best in two scenarios. First, during periods of consolidation when the price is moving steadily sideways, you can often have your bid filled on normal fluctuations without buying at the current market price. Secondly, if you analyze the chart and expect the price to move somewhat lower, you can set a buy order near your predicted bottom, before an expected reversal. Support and resistance levels will play a key factor here. If prices are dropping rapidly for some reason, find out why first, and avoid catching a "falling knife." A falling knife refers to getting caught entering a position when prices are quickly falling, outside of day-to-day fluctuations. In these scenarios, the bottom can be much lower and sustained than anticipated. On the other hand, if you find that your chart looks bullish or may have an upward price movement in the near future, it may be better to set an order that will fill sooner rather than later, as you may end up buying in at a higher price.

By this stage, I recommend having a hardware wallet to move your coins off of the exchange and into your own cold storage. Once you have set up your personal hardware wallet, you should be able to understand how things are stored to a better extent than I can explain here. If you are storing Ether or an ERC token, I recommend using *myetherwallet.com*. This website will work with your hardware wallet and is just used as a cleaner interface to interact with the blockchain. Your tokens do not actually sit on the website.

For any other non-Ethereum-based tokens, Ledger and Trezor both offer desktop apps known as Ledger Live and Trezor Bridge respectively. If the coin you have is not yet supported on the device of your choosing, you can either leave it on the exchange until support is added, or you can download the wallet directly from the coin's website. In this case, your private keys will be held on your machine, and not on your more-secure hardware wallet. However, in most cases you should be able to generate a wallet for the coin of your choosing directly on the desktop app of your hardware wallet.

From there, simply transfer the coin you have just purchased from the exchange onto your cold storage wallet, following the same steps mentioned earlier. Once your transaction has confirmed and appears in your wallet, you are free to disconnect the device and put it somewhere for safe-keeping. Note that disconnecting the device before seeing the coins appear in the wallet has no negative effect on the transfer, other than your peace of mind. Again, this device allows you to interact with the blockchain stored across thousands of computers worldwide, but does not actually physically hold the coins which you are storing.

It may take a few weeks, a few months or even years for an investment to reach an all-time high, but when your investment starts to pay off, begin to take profit along the way to the top rather than after. A good rule of thumb is that after you see a 2x or 3x return, take your initial investment out and let the rest ride up. This method ensures you have locked in gains and can profit from the rest worry-free.

You can take these gains and keep them in BTC/ETH for the long term if you do not need the money immediately, or convert them back to fiat if you feel more comfortable doing so. You can also convert your profits into a stablecoin if you wish to have control of it outside of a centralized bank. There are a couple debit cards available that allow you to spend your crypto without converting to fiat, such as the shift card from Coinbase, but again, this requires that you hold the coins in a Coinbase wallet rather than a personal wallet where you control the private keys. Other companies such as Monaco and TenX are also expected to be releasing crypto debit cards. If you would like to use this method, only keep as much in your hot wallet as you need to spend.

There are still other ways to make money in the cryptocurrency space besides investing in coins and waiting for returns. As we have already discussed, any coin with a PoW algorithm can be mined and any coin with a PoS algorithm can be staked. Both of these actions can generate passive income as long as the coin holds its value. Bitmain is currently the only company which sells ASIC miners, and for ASIC-resistant coins, GPU mining rigs can be set up at home.

Before going this route, I would highly suggest spending some time to research if it is a right fit for you. Mining requires a decent investment into physical hardware in order to provide substantial passive income. They also generate a lot of heat and nose, as well as a high electricity bill. There are multiple websites which provide ROI calculators based on your miner's hashing power as well as your electricity costs. For more information on this visit: *nicehash.com/profitability-calculator* or *cryptocompare.com*

For more advanced traders, websites such as Bitmex offer leveraged trading. This in my opinion is one of the riskiest entrances into the space, and I do not recommend it for the average user. Leveraged trading allows you to trade long or short with up to 100x more money than you actually have. For example, if you have .1 BTC, Bitmex allows you to capitalize off the price volatility of various coins, and take profits as though you were trading with 5x, 25x, 50x or even 100x more than the current USD value of your .1 Bitcoin. However, the higher leverage you use, the more risk you run of getting margin called. In this case, you would lose the amount of your portfolio that you had put forth on a specific trade entry. On a 5x leverage you have a lot more room for price fluctuations before getting margin called, as opposed to a 50x or 100x leverage, where you could be liquidated within a very small percentage move against the direction you traded in.

Being an early adopter in the cryptocurrency space is not for everyone. For those who decide to get involved, understand that there is a learning curve. It can initially be overwhelming, but this feeling will quickly be overcome by anyone with some level of adeptness to use computers and technology in general. Everyone will enter with different risk tolerances and financial circumstances, but for anyone with a bit of time and money on their hands, I think this market is worth investigating. Perhaps for the more risk-averse user wanting to dip their feet in the market, without spending hours and hours on research, it would be more advisable to accumulate some of the high-cap coins periodically and hold for the long term. If you fall into this category, as I believe most people will, you may consider setting aside some money each month as you see fit, and dollar-cost-average into Bitcoin or a few high-cap altcoins with less volatility.

Chapter 10
FINAL THOUGHTS

In the coming years, I believe that as the awareness and understanding of cryptocurrency grows, its adoption and use will increase exponentially. We are currently at a speculation stage where a lot of the price movement is driven by hype rather than fundamentals and real-world adoption. Cryptocurrencies and blockchain technology allow for the borderless transfer of value, instantly to anywhere in the world, without the fees or restrictions of a third party. It favors truth and liberty over state sanctioned power, and eventually will not have to be converted into the local currency, as it is the people's money, not the local government's. It is a global currency with the convenience of being trustless, permissionless, and decentralized. It does not require giving your trust to any entity to complete transactions or conversions. It does not require the permission or approval of any central bank or government to use. No central authority can control its use.

Beyond the convenience that this offers, being your own bank will lead to true financial freedom, if adopted on a wide scale. With individuals being in control of their money, rather than banks, we will observe a huge shift in power for developing countries and developed ones alike. This shift will take power away from governments and banks, and place it back into the hands of the people.

There are currently two billion unbanked people across the world, mostly residing in the Middle East, Sub-Saharan Africa, Latin America, the Caribbean, Europe, Central Asia, and Asia-Pacific. The use of cryptocurrency will allow these people the opportunity to participate in the global financial market, as well as the ability to connect with businesses and institutions around the world. This will strengthen the world economy on a scale never seen before. Understand that you and those around you now have true control over your wealth. Your money no longer has to sit in the hands of those who only have their own interests at heart.

I am of the opinion that banks are at the crux of the rigged financial system in America. We have already seen that actions such as the devaluation of the dollar have made it more difficult to acquire wealth. However, there are many other ways that people with less money are penalized by banks. This can manifest in ways that are as subtle as a $35 overdraft fee or a $5 minimum balance fee. It can also be manifested in ways as abhorrent as a subprime mortgage which carries higher interest rates, higher closing costs, and higher down payments. When all of these factors are added onto the financial burden of those who already struggle, we have the housing crash of 2008. Many people who were given subprime loans ended up paying much more than their home was worth, and eventually defaulted on their mortgage payments.

Meanwhile, the same banks that caused this crash to happen in the first place were able to repossess these homes, and faced no punishment for the economic damage they had caused. They were even rewarded with a bailout (financial reimbursement), for the repercussions of their own recklessness. For the first time, people from all over the world have the ability to take back the financial power which was hijacked from them by governments and banks.

To this same point, one excellent and obvious application of blockchain technology, outside of just cryptocurrency, would be voting. While I do not ever see this coming into fruition without a large scale political revolution, voting on a public blockchain would completely eliminate voter fraud and allow everyone to see the results in a fair and open manner. There are already DApps which allow IDs to be stored on the blockchain, and this could be implemented by governments to be used in political elections, while still having sensitive information remain private. Aside from being infinitely more cost effective and fair, it would also make for higher voter percentages as everything could be performed conveniently from a smartphone or computer. No parties, no electoral college, just individuals recording their votes in a transparent and tamper-proof system.

In closing, I would like to make it very clear that cryptocurrency is only the tip of the iceberg in the ways that blockchain technology can change how we live our lives. Smart contracts and distributed ledger technology also have the ability to make our lives far more efficient and seamless. Imagine walking into a restaurant, ordering food, and simply walking out without ever requesting, waiting for, or handling a bill. Imagine shopping for clothes, picking up the items you'd like, and leaving without ever waiting in a crowded line. RFID tags and other sensors would interpret what is happening in the world around you, and payments would automatically be processed from your cryptocurrency wallet of choice. This could all be a reality with the implementation and use of smart contracts by businesses.

To take this even further, imagine that while purchasing groceries you could simply scan a QR code and get 100% reliable information on exactly which farm a certain meat came from, or even where vegetables were grown. Imagine having your car ownership be recorded on a blockchain and having yearly registration fees be completely eliminated. If your home detected any earthquake or hurricane damage, a smart contract could immediately pay out an insurance claim.

Fun fact: Dubai is on track to become the world's first blockchain-powered city by 2020.

Distributed ledger technology even has the ability to completely eradicate censorship and provide true net neutrality. Rather than websites being hosted through large centralized servers, the data which provides access to websites could be encrypted and distributed to machines (or nodes) throughout the world. Internet service providers (ISPs) would no longer have the power to slow down or throttle any website on the internet. Governments would no longer have the power to place firewalls or censor content. Decentralized social-media sites could even be built where corporations no longer have the power to collect and sell user data to the highest-bidding advertiser. The people who use the internet would have complete control over their online presence.

The possibilities presented by blockchain technology are endless, and have the power to connect the world in a decentralized and trustless way that we have never witnessed before. The blockchain revolution has the potential to eclipse all previous technological revolutions because it is a fundamental revamping of the structure of money itself, as well as the way we trust and conduct business. It may prove to be the single biggest transfer of wealth seen in human history, from those who refuse to accept the new system, to early adopters. I wish I could explain in detail every nuance and intricacy of all the different relevant coins and projects, and tell you which ones will succeed in the long run. The truth is, no one knows for sure. Developments in this space move rapidly and new technologies are constantly evolving. The top 50 coins right now could be replaced in the next 5 years by even better projects. One thing is for sure though, this technology will eventually be the replacement to our current financial system. It may initially coexist, but make no mistake, the revolution is approaching and it will be an outright replacement to the legacy financial systems.

Let this book not be your all-inclusive hub for knowledge of cryptocurrency. Rather I hope that it has served you in laying the groundwork for understanding the fundamentals of the new economy. If this is the future of money and communication, being an early adopter will prove to be quite profitable in the coming years. Time will tell.

Cryptocurrency Resources

Price Tracking

Coinmarketcap.com
Blockfolio
Delta

News

CCN.com
CoinDesk.com
CoinTelegraph.com
Reddit.com/r/CryptoCurrency

Cold Storage Wallets

Ledger: Nano S
Trezor: One / Model T

Mobile / Hot Wallets

Abra Global
BitPay
Coinbase
Enjin
Ethos
Exodus (Desktop)

Fiat-to-Crypto Exchanges

Abra Global
Coinbase

Crypto-to-Crypto Exchanges

Binance
Bitmex
Bittrex

ICO Calendars / Reviews

Coinschedule.com
Crushcrypto.com
ICOBench.com
Reddit.com/r/icocrypto

Mining Info / Profitability

Buybitcoinworldwide.com/mining/calculator
Cryptocompare.com
Nicehash.com/profitability-calculator
Slushpool.com

Staking Info / Profitability

Masternodes.online
Stakingrewards.com

Block Explorers

Bitcoin: Blockchain.com/explorer
Ethereum: Etherscan.io
Litecoin: Live.blockcypher.com/ltc
Monero: Moneroblocks.info

Misc

Bitcoin.org/bitcoin.pdf
Hyperledger.org
Entethalliance.org
Github.com/ethereum/EIPS

Support
The Blockchain Revolution

If you have found value in this reading and decide to dive into the world of cryptocurrency, please consider using the following links when doing so. Your support is very much appreciated.

Coinbase: bit.ly/tbrCoinbase Sign up to Coinbase using this link to receive $10 worth of free Bitcoin after your first $100 purchase

Ledger Wallet: bit.ly/tbrLedger Purchase a Ledger Nano S cold-storage wallet to safely store your cryptocurrency.

Trezor Wallet: bit.ly/tbrTrezor Purchase a Trezor One or a Trezor Model T to safely store your cryptocurrency.

Binance Exchange: bit.ly/tbrBinance Trade your first cryptocurrency using Binance, the most recommended crypto-to-crypto exchange.

Cryptocurrency Glossary

Address: The public identity of a cryptocurrency wallet, where coins can be sent to and from. It appears in the form of a string of letters and numbers and can be shared in plain text or through a QR code. This is the hashed or shortened version of a public key.

Altcoin: Anything that is not Bitcoin. It is debated whether Ethereum should quality as an altcoin or not, because of its place as number two in terms of market cap, and its reputation within the community. However, this this term is arbitrary.

API: Application programming interface. A set of guidelines, communication protocols, and tools for building and operating software. It allows two applications to talk to each other.

ASIC: Application specific integrated circuit. A machine made with the sole purpose of mining a specific cryptocurrency, or multiple cryptocurrencies which share the same mining algorithm.

ATH: All-time high. The highest price that a cryptocurrency has reached.

ATL: All-time low. The lowest price that a cryptocurrency has reached.

Atomic Swap: A method of directly exchanging one type of cryptocurrency for another which may be on a different blockchain. This can be conducted on-chain or off-chain without the use of a centralized third party.

Bag: A bag or bags refers to purchasing an amount of a coin or token to incorporate into one's portfolio.

Bear: A person with the expectation of decreasing prices. This person is known as "bearish" about the market or price.

Blockchain: Distributed public ledgers. Decentralized public databases that everyone can access and read. This is an indestructible and growing list of records, divided into blocks, which are linked together using cryptography.

Block Height: The total number of blocks in a chain up to this point.

Block Reward: The incentive for a miner who successfully calculates a valid hash in a block. This reward also insures that the miners continue to act in the best interest of the blockchain, by securing the network rather than hacking it.

Bots: Automated trading software that can execute trade orders extremely quickly, based on a protocol of buy and sell rules.

Bull: A person with the expectation of increasing prices. This person is known to be "bullish" about the market or price.

Candles: Short for candlesticks. This is a graphing technique used to show changes in price over time such as 5 minutes, 10 minutes, 15 minutes and so on. There can also be daily and weekly candles. Each candle contains 4 points of information: an opening price, closing price, high and low.

Capitulation: Extremely high volume, sharp price declines usually lead by fear (see panic selling). Sellers during this time are willing to give up previous gains, in order to exit the market quickly.

Crypto Twitter: A community of users on Twitter, dedicated to talking about different cryptocurrencies.

Cold Storage: Moving cryptocurrency "offline" to a hardware wallet. This device stores your private keys and has no connection to the internet.

DDoS: Distributed Denial of Service. A cyber-attack in which the perpetrator seeks to make a network resource unavailable, and disrupts the services of a host connected to the internet. This is done by overloading the system with requests, so that legitimate requests cannot be served.

Dead Cat Bounce: A sharp upward movement in price, occurring after a steep decline. This movement is temporary, and is exhausted quickly, before further downward movement.

DYOR: "Do Your Own Research." Don't just take people for their word.

Exchange: A business which allows customers to trade cryptocurrencies for fiat money or other cryptocurrencies.

Exchange Token: A token (usually ERC20) issued by a cryptocurrency exchange which grants the holder certain rights within the platform such a voting, dividends, or trading fee discounts.

Fiat: Currency that is government issued legal tender such as the USD, CAD or EUR.

First-Mover Advantage: An intrinsic advantage, experienced by an innovator or pioneer in a specific field, as a result of greater experience and market acceptance, as compared to competitors. This is similar to starting a race early.

FOMO: Fear of missing out.

Fork: A fork or chain-split creates an alternate version of a blockchain with modified protocols.

Fungible: Mutually interchangeable or the same. Able to replace or be replaced by another identical item.

FUD: Fear, uncertainty and doubt. Propaganda and media coverage spread in order to lower investor confidence and drop market prices.

Gas: The fee for any operation performed on the Ethereum network. The gas limit refers to the maximum amount of gas a user is willing to spend on a transaction. The gas price refers to the price you are willing to pay for a transaction. Setting a higher gas price incentivizes miners to prioritize a transaction, and results in a faster confirmation.

Gwei: The denomination used in defining the cost of gas in transactions on the Ethereum network.

HODL: An intentional misspelling of the world "hold". Coined from a thread on bitcointalk, this term refers to a passive investment strategy that entails holding a coin through the short-term dips and pumps, in order to reap the long-term price gains.

ICO: Initial Coin Offering. A type of crowdfunding, similar to when a company has an initial public offering of a stock. This money is used to fund business expenses such as hiring developers, marketing, exchange listings and various partnerships.

IoT: Internet of Things. An ecosystem of connected physical objects, accessible through the internet.

KYC: Know-Your-Customer. A process which refers to a financial institution's obligation to verify the identity of a customer, in line with global anti-money-laundering (AML) laws.

Limit Order: Orders placed by traders to execute the buying or selling of a cryptocurrency, only when a certain price is reached.

Mainnet: An independent blockchain, running on its own proprietary network.

Market Capitalization: The total market value of a cryptocurrency. This is found by taking the supply of a coin multiplied by its price. (Ex. 21 million Bitcoin x $10,000 = $210,000,000,000 market cap.)

Market Order: Orders placed by traders to execute the buying or selling of a cryptocurrency at the current best available price.

Masternode: A server maintained by its owner, similar to full nodes, but with additional functionalities such as anonymizing transactions, clearing transactions and participating in governance and voting. It was initially popularized by Dash to reward owners for their contribution to the network.

Mining: The process of completing mathematical algorithms through computer hardware, in order to confirm legitimate transactions and write new blocks.

Moon: A situation where the price of a cryptocurrency moves up extremely high in a short amount of time (mooning).

Multi-Sig: A multi-signature wallet requires more than one private key to authorize a transaction.

Node: A computer with a copy of a blockchain.

Oracle: An aggregator and verifier of information, which links real-world data to the blockchain, by allowing it to interact with smart contracts.

OTC: Over-the-counter trading occurs outside of exchanges, and typically involves buying and selling large quantities at a set price. This process usually involves a custodial, which acts as an intermediary between two parties who wish to trade.

Panic Selling: The selling of large quantities of an asset (relative to one's portfolio) due to sudden fear of declining prices. This can arise from the expectation of a drop in demand or market value, and can refer to an individual or group of people.

P&D: Pump and dump. Schemes which attempt to boost the price of a coin through order book manipulation, and fomo based on exaggerated statements, in order to sell to unsuspecting buyers.

Permissionless: The absence of the need to ask for permission from a central figure, in order to complete an action.

PoS: Proof-of-Stake. A type of algorithm by which a cryptocurrency blockchain aims to achieve distributed consensus, and choose the creator of the next block, based on how many coins they hold.

PoW: Proof-of-Work. A type of algorithm used to validate transactions, deter denial of service attacks and other abuses on the blockchain, by requiring work from the service requestor.

Protocol: The set of rules which define interactions on a network.

ROI: Return on investment. Percentage gains from the initial invested amount.

Satoshi: Named after the alleged creator of Bitcoin, Satoshi Nakamoto, a Satoshi is one hundred millionth of a Bitcoin; this is its smallest denomination. One Satoshi = 0.00000001 Bitcoin.

Seg-Wit: Segregated witness is a Bitcoin improvement proposal (BIP) designed to fix transaction malleability. It separates the signature from the block content, which had the side effect of reducing individual transaction sizes and allowing for second-layer solutions.

Signature: A cryptographic signature is a mathematical algorithm that allows an individual to prove ownership of something. When your Bitcoin software signs a transaction with the private key, the entire network can see that the signature matches the wallet address from which Bitcoins are being spent. It is mathematically impossible to derive someone's private key from a wallet address.

Smart Contract: A computer program which sits on a blockchain and performs an action, after specific requirements are met.

Staking: Holding Proof-of-Stake coins in a wallet, in order to receive block rewards.

TA: Technical Analysis. Analyzing statistics and patterns, gathered from trading activities, in an attempt to forecast future price movement.

Testnet: An alternative blockchain used by developers for testing.

Ticker Symbol: A shortened name for a traded commodity ($BTC/BTC).

Trustless: An absence of the necessity to trust the counterparty with whom you are interacting with, in order for transactions to be enforced as intended.

Wallet: Software program that stores public and private keys, to interact with various blockchains. A hot wallet is connected to the internet while a cold wallet is offline.

Whale: People or groups that have large quantities of cryptocurrency.

Whitepaper: A persuasive, authoritative, in-depth report on a specific topic that informs readers about a complex issue, and provides a solution and roadmap. This document is typically prepared by an ICO team to interest investors in their project.

Made in the USA
Coppell, TX
04 December 2020